Out of the Shadows

8 23 2020

Out of the Shadows

**Out of the Shadows**

**as seen through selected servant**

**Charles E. Hobbs**

Hideaway Publishing Company

Out of the Shadows

Out of the Shadows

## Table of Contents

Chapter 0 . . . . . . . . . . . . . . . . . . . . . . . . . . . . . Page 7
Chapter 1 . . . . . . . . . . . . . . . . . . . . . . . . . . . . . Page 16
Chapter 2 . . . . . . . . . . . . . . . . . . . . . . . . . . . . . Page 32
Chapter 3 . . . . . . . . . . . . . . . . . . . . . . . . . . . . . Page 81
Chapter 4 . . . . . . . . . . . . . . . . . . . . . . . . . . . . . Page 159
Chapter 5 . . . . . . . . . . . . . . . . . . . . . . . . . . . . . Page 176
Chapter 6 . . . . . . . . . . . . . . . . . . . . . . . . . . . . . Page 194
Chapter 7 . . . . . . . . . . . . . . . . . . . . . . . . . . . . . Page 214

Out of the Shadows

## Chapter 0

### *The Beginning*

**In the Beginning:** The Committee of three met in the present age. As always, they meet in agreement as One. The Committee considered their major creation of Adam in their image in the beginning. Their desire was for the generations that resulted from Adam and Eve to understand the truth. The truth about the love that the Committee had for each individual descendant has now been shown throughout the ages. The Committee's plan for the ages resulted from foreknowledge of the love that Adam portrayed for Eve. The love of Adam for Eve supported the plan the Committee has developed out of the Committee's love for the created image and descendants. The truth that supported the Committee's plan of love included their need of perfection. *Love with mercy and justice stands as the created goal included in the Committee's plan.*

The Committee discussed that most descendants of Adam know the basic story of the temptation by Satan in the garden when dealing with Eve. After Eve was tempted, most of the descendants fail to understand the truth known by the Committee with their great understanding of love. The generations of descendants often recognize the law given to Moses and the two basic love commandments. The two commandments are to love God above all else and to love fellow persons as an individual loves one's self. These commandments are to be fulfilled by one's free-will decision. *(The Committee noted that these two commandments indicate nothing about God's (the Committee's) love for the created image and descendants. The truth of the Committee's plan of love for mankind (male and female) is revealed in the Word. To indicate this love is a goal of the Committee in this meeting.)* The individual free-will becomes one's self-will and actions that follow are under the control of the individual and not control of the Committee. This last sentence indicates one of the great truths of the Word. Hence, the truth is that all individual descendant's actions are determined by that individual and not by the Committee.

The truth in the Word is that Eve's and Adam's decisions were determined by themselves. Eve yielded to the temptation by Satan. However, Adam was not tempted by Satan. Most generational individuals do not recognize what actually happened in the garden. (Hidden in the Word is this truth presented by the inspired presentation by Paul.) Adam had a choice between the two love commandments. Adam followed the second commandment of love. He had true love for Eve and that led him of his own free-will to sacrifice himself to sin. Thus, the Adamic sin originated out of love and sacrifice which the Committee through love understood. However, justice was demanded as well as mercy. This need by the Committee along with their love for the created image (Adam) and the following descendants resulted in the great plan of salvation. A substitute was needed to show both justice and mercy. Hence, the plan developed as shown in the Word. The truth of the plan follows as the Committee tries to reveal the plan so all descendants can understand. The truth is that Adam's decision and action forms the need for the plan of love designed by the Committee. One of the Committee to be known as the second Adam in the Word came as a sacrifice substitute for the created image and all descendants. Through love Jesus (as the second Adam) came as a substitute for all individual descendants as evidenced by the Word. The plan is revealed through history of prophecy and mystery as designed. History reveals the truth found in the Word. A great portion of the plan is revealed in the following as the truth moves **_out of the shadows_**. _The Committee desires that all individual descendants of the created image recognize that each descendant is created in the image of the Committee. As a result, each descendant has an innate desire for love rather than hate as presented in many lives. Love is a goal beyond hate. Free-will to choose is a responsibility left to each descendant image of creation as a gift from the creators. Self-control of self-will is the responsibility of each individual descendant._

**As recorded in the Word:** Adam was not tempted by Satan. Adam loved his wife and chose of his own freewill to hearken to her and chose to be with her but still had disobeyed the Committee. The Committee understood Adam's show of love and sacrifice. Therefore, out of love for the created image, the Committee through foreknowledge had designed a plan that includes both mercy and justice. The plan is revealed in the Word of truth as follows.

> Genesis 3:17 kjv 17 And unto Adam he said, Because *thou hast hearkened unto the voice of thy wife*, and hast eaten of the tree, of which I commanded thee, saying, Thou shalt not eat of it: cursed is the ground for thy sake; in sorrow shalt thou eat of it all the days of thy life;

*A hidden shadow of the future plan was shown in the garden; A death and sacrifice was a hidden shadow of a future death and sacrifice on the cross.*

> Genesis 3:21 kjv 21 Unto Adam also and to his wife did the LORD God make coats of skins, and clothed them.
> 1 Timothy 2:13-14 kjv 13 For Adam was first formed, then Eve. 14 *And Adam was not deceived*, but the *woman being deceived* was in the transgression.
> 1 Corinthians 15:22 kjv 22 For as in Adam all die, even so in Christ shall all be made alive.
> 1 Corinthians 15:45 kjv 45 And so it is written, The first man Adam was made a living soul; the last Adam was made a quickening spirit.

As the descendants of Adam check out the truth and plan that follows, the Committee wants to reveal their love for all individual descendants. The Committee continues to desire that the created descendants recognize the love for the creation from God (the Committee).

> 1 John 4:7-8 kjv 7Beloved, let us love one another: for *love is of God*; and everyone that loveth is born of God, and knoweth God. 8He that loveth not knoweth not God; for *God is love*.

The Committee has stayed in touch continually since their last meeting. Nothing has changed in their designed plan as far as they could discern since their first meeting and their designed plan for their new creation. Their foreknowledge of being able to plan while knowing the beginning from the end and being able to see the end from the beginning had been a definite guide to their perfect plan. Now after a little over 6000 mankind years they decided to review the plan. They met to open their recorded plan and to discuss some of their design and see where they were as their plan continues to be sure but also open ended to some extent. They had recorded their plan with a characteristic provided to their new creation that they did not control so they had with foreknowledge created changes in strategies based on the characteristic that came to be known as free will. Their intent was to 1. Discuss the intent of the plan, 2. Discuss the guide to their plan, 3. Discuss the three-prong truth in their plan, 4. Discuss the current status, and 5. Discuss the Committee's longsuffering characteristic in relation to the current and future status. The Committee agreed to focus on the plan as it was observed up to the present time and then to consider an additional meeting that would discuss more specific details of the plan from the present into the future.

(As usual, their agreement was as One and they knew that mankind had studied the record with the leadership of One of them and had now noted most of the events the Committee had planned due to the passage of time. They also recognized that many of mankind had no idea of the events that had been planned.)

General Guide: 2 Timothy 2:15

<sub>2 Timothy 2:15 kjv 15</sub>Study to shew thyself approved unto God, a workman that needeth not to be ashamed, <u>*rightly dividing the word of truth.*</u>

The plan focused on revealing the Committee and the plan to mankind. The One member of the Committee that now had a glorified body had revealed to mankind the overall plan of prophecy. The plan of prophecy was and is <u>to tell the events of history ahead of time so that when the events happen mankind should believe and understand.</u>

The Committee had planned on using the major characteristics in how mankind learned. The telling of history ahead of time was recorded as the written Word. The prophesied historical happenings were for mankind to experience during the present. Experience of what had been prophesied ahead of time was intended to be a teacher and continues to be a major teacher. Time revealed past and present experiences unfolding for each generation of mankind.

The Committee agreed to discuss the plan based on the following divisions during this present meeting. The Committee recognized that because of the interwoven hidden messages in the recorded Word, the three divisions would overlap in some cases.

***Truth 0: Original Planning – Before the Beginning:*** The truths will be expanded as the Committee meeting is discussed and recorded.

***Truth 1: Prophecy of the gentile nations and the nation of Israel.*** The Committee had now completed much of the prophetic sequence. The future of the nations with focus on Israel has been told ahead of time in the Word. Most of the prophetic events related to the nations has now happened. Mankind can now see that the Committee has provided substance to support belief in the Committee and as Jesus has stated, *the plan was and continues to be when mankind sees the prophecy come to pass, mankind should develop substance and evidence to believe through faith.*

> Hebrews 11:1 kjv 1Now **faith is** the **substance** of things hoped for, the **evidence** of **things not seen.**

> John 14:29 kjv 29And now I have told you before it come to pass, that, when it is come to pass, ye might believe.

***Truth 2: Prophecy revealing the coming Messiah as Jesus the Christ.*** The Committee has now revealed in the written Word facts about the physical life of the coming Messiah of Israel. Facts related to the suffering Messiah and His physical life has been presented and fulfilled. The

13

plan continued . . . to tell the future ahead of time so when the events came to pass in the fulness of time . . . mankind would have substance and evidence to believe in Jesus as the true sacrifice for receiving forgiveness for the Adamic sin as Abraham did through belief before the true sacrifice.  As the Committee had planned, <u>there was and is only one way to receive a covering of righteousness as Abraham did before the Law through Moses was given as a guide.  The plan continues to be when mankind saw the Committee's ability to provide prophecy that would come to pass, mankind should have substance and evidence to believe through faith.</u>

> Genesis 15:6 kjv  6And he believed in the LORD; and he counted it to him for righteousness.

He is Abraham in the above written Word.

> John 14:29 kjv 29And now I have told you before it come to pass, that, when it is come to pass, ye might believe.

The speaker is Jesus in the above written Word.

**_Truth 3:  The mystery of the Church Age._**  (With all the support and evidence of Jesus as the Messiah that suffered, He became the sacrifice for all, was buried, resurrected, reappeared, and could have set up the expected Kingdom . . . but, Israel as a whole rejected Him at the selected time.  This ushered in the present time planned by the Committee to provide an opportunity for the Gentiles to accept the atonement for sins through the same belief in Jesus and His accomplishments as planned for Israel.  This present age has been introduced through

Paul's teaching and is presently still in progress. The mystery of this age continues to be revealed.)

## Chapter I

### *Truth 0: Original Planning – Before the Beginning*

***Once upon a time (before the beginning):*** The Committee of three met as One and developed an overall plan that needed a set of creatures developed to love in their huge strategic plan. The preplanning was used in development of a later more involved plan. The set of creatures to be developed in the preplan was to be less superior to the characteristics of the main planned creation but have certain desirable characteristics. These preplanned creatures were to be known as angels. The Committee developed these creatures with a free will to make decisions and were designed to serve and minister to the Committee much like future robots to be developed by a created image. However, as pre-known and planned by the Committee, the free will and a trait known as envy resulted in a rebellion so that a portion of the angelic beings followed a well-endowed leader named Lucifer. The Committee then continued to develop the more strategic plan to create a new image in order to get the needed images to love the Committee as the created images were loved by the Committee. (The Committee had determined that they desired an object to love and desired to be loved in return. They wanted the created image to also have this desire.) An original special image was created in the Committee's own image and selected to the desired object of the Committee's love. The desired trait was a part of this special creation. The Committee recognized that the true love desired from the created image was using the decision of love toward the Committee based on free will . . . a special trait given to the new image. This new image was planned and to be known as mankind (male and female).

The Committee discussed how from the beginning they had known the need for the created image and the descendants to recognize the spiritual realm and decide to return the Committee's love or not to return the Committee's love based on a free will decision rather than by force. They decided to record and explain their attempts to provide mankind evidence of the Committee's invisible existence along with their caring love toward mankind.

The plan was focused originally on One of the Committee to be the Communicator from the Committee toward mankind and to be recognized as the Creator.

The Christ (Messiah), the designated Communicator to mankind said to Moses: Tell them "I AM" sent you. See Exodus 3:14 in kjv (King James Version) of the Bible. Jesus (the chosen One as Creator and Messiah) also told His disciples in the New Testament in words similar to: I will tell you now so that when it happens, you will believe. John: 14:29 kjv. This last verse indicates a portion of the Committee's plan for mankind to know and understand.

Exodus 3:14 kjv 14 And God said unto Moses, I AM THAT I AM: and he said, Thus shalt thou say unto the children of Israel, I AM hath sent me unto you

John 13:19 kjv 19 Now I tell you before it come, that, when it is come to pass, ye may believe that I am *he*.

John 14:29 kjv 29 And now I have told you before it come to pass, that, when it is come to pass, ye might believe.

John 16:4 kjv 4 But these things have I told you, that when the time shall come, ye may remember that I told you of them. And these things I said not unto you at the beginning, because I was with you.

Matthew 24:24-25 kjv 24 For there shall arise false Christs, and false prophets, and shall shew great signs and wonders; insomuch that, if it were possible, they shall deceive the very elect. 25 Behold, I have told you before.

The Committee noted that repeating a saying three times in the Written Word meant it was important. Jesus had repeated this plan three times. They also noted that three witnesses established a definite truth. (The Committee noted that they were and are three in One as known to mankind to be God. This establishes the Truth in the Word. This witness is to be discussed later in this recording as presented in the Word.)

**To Start the Beginning**: The Committee had met and decided on ONE basic plan: *To provide evidence of the unseen so that the seen would reflect the true existence of the unseen continued to be a major part of the plan.* Some evidence had now been verified, offered, and used by mankind. Three basic examples noted by the Committee are: The wind which has always been known by seen results but unseen by the natural innate abilities of mankind. The wind has been accepted by mankind not because it is seen, but evidence by observing of the representation of leaves that move and are seen along with other seen results of the unseen (Some wind was considered good as the cool breezes and some wind was considered terrible such as storms and tornados). (The Committee noted evidence of the unseen led to belief in the unseen wind.) Hence, mankind has learned the reality of the unseen (good and bad) by the evidence provided by the seen results of the existing unseen but existing phenomena. The Committee discussed some more of this evidence of the unseen that has been accepted has been: Unseen radio waves that are substantiated through detection and used in a variety of ways as evidence of the unseen; X-rays that are substantiated through detection and used in a variety of ways as evidence of the unseen; Unseen smaller mass particles that are substantiated through detection of paths through clouds when the particles are so small to defy the sight of mankind. Mankind has used a variety of ways to see the unseen in their mind's eye. The Committee planned on mankind to recognize the unseen existence of spiritual realm and the Committee in a similar revealing of events through time. The Committee recognized their created image (in their own likeness) would have the ability to detect the evidence of the unseen existence in a variety of ways. Thus. the plan as developed was to use mankind's ability and to guide with appropriate evidence of the unseen. The Committee noted this ability to use and recognize the unseen substances within the real world as one of the major reasons mankind has been able to adapt to the unseen and seen changes and to use this ability to not become extinct as many animals and plants have become extinct or adapted in past history. Learning from previous historical events already passed has been planned as a great value to mankind. Making correct decisions in handling and accepting the unseen by looking at the results and reacting to the circumstances has been another ability that had been planned to be beneficial in continued use within the seen world of existence.

The Committee decided to review examples they had planned so mankind would recognize the existence of the Committee and their planned connection between the Committee in the unseen existence and the created images (mankind) in their seen real world. The examples planned were usually physical events for mankind to experience. These events were planned to provide the foundation of the acceptance of the unseen by looking at the evidence shown by the following observed (seeing evidence of the unseen) plan of the Committee.

**Once Upon a Time** in the beginning . . . The Committee of three agreed as One to create a physical environment to provide a habitation for an image to be created in their image within a physical tabernacle to be recognized as a human body. They planned on having an image that would provide fellowship with them and an image that they could share their love with. The creation of this environment and the inhabitants (plants and animals) of the environment were designed and completed as recorded in the written Word. After the environment and the inhabitants were created One of the Committee (named Christ) was given the responsibility of creating and communicating directly with the newly created image (named Adam). A special help mate was also created (named Eve). Adam and Eve were put in charge of all the created environment and inhabitants. (recorded for mankind in a book called the Bible -Genesis 1-3). Then, began the attempt to share love with the created images. The Committee had recognized the need to provide for a free choice for mankind in sharing of the love. The free will to make decisions was built into the created images. The environment was basic and contained entities that were descriptive (such as earthly, three-dimensional space, and time as a fourth dimension) and the living inhabitants (animals and plants). The choice was made by the Committee to love the created image but also of great importance was that the created images and descendants (as the created images and descendants were made to reproduce) show that they made independent individual choices to love the Committee without force. Thus, the free will to make decisions was an important attribute of the created images. A strategic plan was to be detailed and it had been, and the results were now to be reviewed.

**The Unveiled Image and Freedom:** To provide a choice by the created images so the created images could show their free choice to love the Committee, a decision to provide an alternative was determined. But the alternative had to be an opponent similar but opposite to the Committee. A determined decision was to be made by the created image to select between the Committee and the alternative. The alternative needed to be one that the created images (men and women) would have an equal free will choice in their decisions. Thus, an element in the creation was determined and called sin. This was an action to not do what the Committee set down as commandments. Two commandments were given. Adam and Eve were to take care of the created environment in the Garden of Eden. However, they were not to eat the fruit of one tree (the Tree of Knowledge of Good and Evil). (Note they could eat of the Tree of Life as a second special tree.)

> Genesis 2:15-17 kjv 15 And the LORD God took the man, and put him into the garden of Eden to dress it and to keep it. 16 And the LORD God commanded the man, saying, Of every tree of the garden thou mayest freely eat: 17 But of the tree of the knowledge of good and evil, thou shalt not eat of it: for in the day that thou eatest thereof thou shalt surely die.

Then created mankind were given a tempter known as Satan (Lucifer) to provide the alternative. Satan was given power to be the alternative needed to entice the images (Adam and Eve) to sin. Of major importance for mankind to select was that Satan also be unseen and be of a spiritual realm as was the Committee. The created angels also had a free will and as members of the spiritual realm they could choose to follow Satan or Christ as the competition developed. Satan had some support with angels that joined Satan and fallen angels (those following Satan) were called demons when supporting Satan. Both Satan and Christ used the opportunity to be seen by mankind although Satan was limited by the Committee during the competition based on a rule that he could not lead mankind using procedures outside mankind's ability to make an educated decision. (One such limitation was indicated and recorded in the Word in relation to Job.)

> Job 1:12 kjv 12 And the LORD said unto Satan, Behold, all that he hath is in thy power; only upon himself put not forth thine hand. So, Satan went forth from the presence of the LORD.

***The field of decision by mankind was protected in fairness between the two spiritual realms (Satan's or Christ's with the spiritual realm of Christ representing the Committee).***

**The Unveiling of What happened:** Satan took the form of a serpent and visited the Garden and Eve. Eve was tempted and ate of the forbidden fruit. Thus. she sinned. When Adam knew that Eve had sinned, he also decided to be with her in the sinful position before the Committee and he made a free will independent decision (not tempted by Satan) to also eat of the fruit. Hence, both Adam and Eve showed a decision to sin and not follow the commandments of love provided to test their love for the Committee. But the great love of the Committee toward the creation was still not broken. The Committee had some hidden plans that the created images (to be mankind) and Satan did not know.

**The Unveiling of the Great Problem:** A problem was to develop the unseen portion of the plan for the redemption of sinful mankind as time progressed. The plan included two unforeseen parts for the redemption of mankind including a plan for the individual redemption of the produced individuals as time progressed.

The Committee wanted the created images (mankind) to produce other images and the Committee knew the production would take some time to produce enough numbers to select love of the Committee when the alternative was also present. The Committee understood the created images.

The Committee also understood how the images (mankind) learned after eating of the Tree of the Knowledge of Good and Evil. Mankind tended to learn by physical things they could see and figure out how the physical things existed (live and inanimate things). The Committee existed of spirits of another dimension and needed that the created images accept this difference. A part of the future hopes of the Committee was that the created images should accept the possibility to become more spiritual and provide the future fellowship desired. The Committee noted that in the present and past as provided for mankind to experience, history had now shown Jesus taking on the special glorified body after a physical death. They noted that the present meeting would also discuss this event being revealed.

**The Unveiling of THE Plan:** Note that use of prophecy continued to be a major component of the plan . . . to tell ahead of time of events to happen so that when the events came to pass mankind would recognize the truth provided by the Committee as _substance and evidence in order to establish individual belief (faith) as desired._

**_In the Beginning . . . And Now later:_**

**The Committee of three always met in agreement as One.** They had met in the beginning and now a little over 6000 man years had passed, and the Committee knew this meeting was toward the ending of time. The plan as determined in the beginning had been unveiled through prophecy and shadows. The result was more and more evident as the Committee had seen the ending from the beginning. They had understood the image they had created, and the free will decisions given to the individuals that would be produced. The plan to show the Committee's invisible existence to mankind had now been unveiled in such a way that mankind had most of the revelation recorded and set before them in a book called the Bible. A major departure of mankind from looking at the plan as recorded had happened and was continuing to happen. Only a few events now remained to be unveiled to complete the plan. The Committee knew that mankind had increased in knowledge with an opportunity to understand the plan more than before. The plan was developed so mankind would have no excuse for not understanding the choice needing to be made of a free will decision. The hidden prophetic historical events were noted and being almost completely fulfilled, and mysteries had now been unveiled. The ending was now to be discussed.

The Committee decided to review some of the planned opportunities for mankind as they had developed the plan so far. The focus was on events that had already happened for mankind to recognize the Committee in order to overcome Satan and obtain righteousness through belief only as Abraham had done. The Committee discussed that works alone did not establish the righteousness needed. The Committee noted that the good works that were needed were done following established faith.

> James 2:18 kjv 18 Yea, a man may say, Thou hast **faith**, and I have **works**: shew me thy **faith without** thy **works**, and I will shew thee my **faith** by my **works**.

> James 2:20 kjv 20 But wilt thou know, O vain man, that **faith without works** is dead?

> James 2:26 kjv 26 For as the body **without** the spirit is dead, so **faith without works** is dead also.

The review follows:

**The Plan:** Now the plan was to create a gradual unveiling of scenarios whereby mankind would recognize the Committee as being real even though they were spiritual and invisible. This unveiling was to be done in a variety of ways that mankind was to observe as they reproduced throughout the ages. Parts of the plan was to be revealed through natural phenomena and parts of the plan was to be revealed as time passed after being told ahead of times. There were several ways to accomplish this in the Committee's plan. A portion of these truths are revealed in the following report.

The most important part of the plan included a method of redemption for mankind based on forgiveness of sin and mankind's acceptance of the plan through individual faith. The Committee discussed the assignment of the One known as Christ and the Son to be the Communicator and the choice between Satan (the alternative) and the Christ (also to be recorded as the Messiah). They recognized this plan as having now been exposed for mankind to recognize, accept, and experience. The prophecy and fulfillment of this portion was recorded in the Word and to be discussed now by the Committee.

Of extreme importance was the recording of the events of unveiling in a record called the Bible. These recorded events were now to be reviewed as mankind had these recorded for their own reviewing. The Committee had directed mankind to teach the Word to their produced generations. The Committee had preserved these events for mankind.

An important part of the Committee's plan was that although the desire was that mankind accept the unseen spiritual realm of the Committee; the alternative opponent Satan did not realize the plan. Thus, Satan was not to understand the entire plan. Hence the challenge for the Committee was to reveal the plan at the correct time to mankind and to Satan but not in previous time to Satan. (I Cor: 2:6-8 kjv) This also provided a challenge to mankind to choose the Committee rather than Satan for some reason. This reason was to recognize the Committee's love for the created images (mankind) and return it of individual mankind's own free will.

1 Corinthians 2: 6-8 kjv 6 Howbeit we speak wisdom among them that are perfect: yet not the wisdom of this world, nor of the princes of this world, that come to nought: 7 But we speak the wisdom of God in a mystery, even the **hidden wisdom, which God**

> **ordained before the world unto our glory: ⁸Which none of the princes of this world knew: for had they known it, they would not have crucified the Lord of glory.**

**The Plan Skeleton**: A plan outline without all the details exposed was created. (In creating a plan, the Committee knew that details would come up based on the free will decisions of mankind and strategy changes would happen and were included in the plan.) The Committee knew the rules (commandments) and developed several strategies to use in order to provide outcomes to influence wisdom of the created images. Recognizing the opponent's (Satan's) ability to develop strategies, the Committee's plan was to reveal truths in the written Word about the Committee's strategies contrasted with the alternative's strategies.

The plan began with testing mankind's individual free will determination to follow the commandments of the Committee. Mankind immediately failed in the Garden of Eden and inherited the Sin of Adam. *(Note that Eve was tempted by the alternative, but Adam made a free will decision to be with Eve rather than follow God of his own free will (Supported by Paul in 1 Timothy 2:14 kjv). Thus, Adam's sin to follow the circumstances rather than the commandments was the Adamic sin that was considered inherited as each of the produced images was to make this kind of choice . . . of their own free will within the individual circumstances. The Committee noted an individual decision based on belief (as Abraham had accomplished) was and is required by mankind to have the righteousness of Jesus substituted for mankind's Adamic sin.)*

> ¹ Timothy 2: 14 kjv ¹⁴And Adam was not deceived, but the woman being deceived was in the transgression.

Now the skeleton of the plan involved the setting up of the strategy that involved natural events and activities to reveal the greater plan (to remain a mystery) but the plan left out some details. Patterns of the unseen was to be provided but the final real result was not to be shown and to remain hidden (Much as mankind provides the plan of a house, but this is not the real house.) Similarly, the Committee had used a method involving shadows to hide some details of their plan until the actual time of fulfillment. The pattern of the shadows was as a shadow of a tree that provided an outline but hid some major details. The true details of the shadow patterns were to be revealed by at least three important procedures.

One was through prophecy of events to come true and a part of this plan was using history of nations throughout the ages. A second event was through the design of natural elements in the creation that mankind would learn. A third strategy was to remain a mystery till Christ at a later time would reveal the greater component for redemption of mankind. As indicated, the strategy continued to include the telling of future events so that when they come true mankind should come to realize the true great strategy (John 14:29 kjv). *A major part of the plan was to provide a recorded account of the plan in a special book (the Bible). The plan would eventually be revealed to mankind and to Satan as time passed. (Most of the plan had now throughout the passage of time been revealed as intended.)*

**Food to Provide Flesh on the Skeleton.** Now the plan included to let some of the details be completed as time passed so mankind would begin to understand the true choice as the strategy was developed. *Remember that the major strategy was and to be continued for mankind to understand the pattern of what is seen in the physical realm and to transcend into a recognition of and acceptance of the unseen spiritual realm including the Committee.*

***Some Meat*:** Prophecy was to be one of the procedures for mankind to understand. The Committee continued to discuss the plan to tell ahead of time what would happen and then let the event happen so mankind should recognize that the Committee knew what was ahead. The Committee's love was to be shown as time proceeded along with a fair judgement and understanding of mankind's weakness toward sin. An important pairing of freedoms along with responsibility in making appropriate decisions was provided for mankind. Freedoms did not stand alone. The pairing with responsibility was a huge companion of freedoms. The Committee noted than mankind seemed to focus on freedoms without a focus on responsibility based on the second commandment as stated in the Word.

> Mark 12:29-31 kjv [29] And Jesus answered him, The first of all the commandments is, Hear, O Israel; The Lord our God is one Lord: [30] And thou shalt love the Lord thy God with all thy heart, and with all thy

soul, and with all thy mind, and with all thy strength: this is the first commandment. ³¹ And the second is like, namely this, Thou shalt love thy neighbour as thyself. There is none other commandment greater than these.

**_Three Focal Points_**: As the clues developed, the plan focused as planned on three major components. One was the destiny of the Israelite nation (along with other nations). One was the coming Messiah. Major clues were given in relation to these first two focal points so that mankind would begin to understand the Committee as planned. The third focal point was to remain a mystery and had now been revealed. These three focal points as planned and now partially or fully completed was to be discussed. The Committee knew that sufficient evidence had been presented so _mankind now had no excuse not to have faith to receive a covering of righteousness as a substitute for sin. Substance and evidence had now been established for individual faith as needed for individual belief followed by appropriate individual Works._

## Chapter II

### *Truth 1: Prophecy*

**Chapter II:** *Truth 1: Prophecy Gentiles and Israel: On the Nations (Israel in focus)*

*The Committee now discussed and looked at the predicted history and its fulfillment throughout time.*

**Two Basic Covenants:** The Committee made note that two basic covenants are national covenants for the specific nation of Israel. The first covenant was established between Abraham and the Communicator with the Communicator representing the Committee. (The Committee recognized the Communicator throughout history to take on different methods to approach mankind. Mankind were to recognize these changing methods also and divide the previous truth from the developing truth.) The new covenant was declared through Jeremiah. These different covenants are each sealed as follows.

*First Covenant:* Between the Communicator and Abraham: This covenant was stated in Genesis 12 and confirmed in Genesis 15 in the Word for mankind to understand. The truth was shown in forms of shadows of the real. Some of the shadows during the Old Testament history was the Tabernacle, priesthood, and sacrifice of the lamb as established by the Communicator providing the law to Moses. The shadows formed bridges between the first covenant and the new covenant. Jeremiah states the new covenant in relation to the shadow of the lamb sacrifice when the nation of Israel was developed through the shadow of moving toward receiving the promised land through the exodus. (This establishment of the sequence of moving from the first covenant for the nation of Israel to the new covenant for a better truth was to support mankind to recognize the improved truth being revealed through time. History provided substance and evidence for mankind to believe in the Committee's plan of redemption from the Adamic sinful state. The latter covenant is to be established for a remnant of Israelites in due time based on true belief in Jesus as the Messiah.)

*Reason:* The reason for the first covenant used to establish the nation of Israel was because mankind had used their free will to continue as a majority to not do the will of the Committee. Mankind as a whole did not return the companionship and obey the commandments as the Committee desired. A continued development of prophetic fulfillments was desired through time for mankind to become more understanding of the relationship desired by the Committee. The first covenant was established after mankind had tried to build the known Tower of Babel. Again, this event was recorded in the Word to support understanding by mankind.

*The Committee made a note that mankind could not reach the doing of the commandments perfectly but belief in*

*Jesus as the Messiah was needed for individual mankind to be forgiven for any lack of trying to obey. Mercy from the Committee was often based on the belief by mankind of Jesus as the Messiah and the earnest trying by mankind to accomplish the commandments. The Committee decided to discuss longsuffering and mercy later in their meeting.*

*The Tower of Babel:* (The Committee noted that there was a different perspective that they hoped mankind would understand as meaning became different throughout time and the events of the past prophecy became true in an extended time period. The past event of the Tower as established was a shadow of some greater truth in the future for mankind to understand. The Communicator (In the human form of Jesus) had expressed this great plan . . *. to tell ahead of time what was going to happen and then when it happened . . . mankind should believe in the Committee*.) For the current time mankind was to recognize the Committee for current events. For the time of the Tower of Babel mankind focused on self and to make a name for self. The Committee recognized this as being a continued problem with mankind to focus on self and self-promotion above the Committee. A truth recognized by the Committee was the created cannot become greater than the creator, This was a given for the Committee, so the Committee did not approve self-promotion to the creator level but did recognize it as a free will development. Hence, they scrambled the languages in the past event of the Tower so mankind could not work together. (The Committee decided to discuss the hidden future of this shadow later but for now the direct happening of this past event being a part of the reason behind the development of the nation of Israel was in focus.)

> Genesis 11:1-9 kjv 11 And the whole earth was of one language, and of one speech. ²And it came to pass, as they journeyed from the east, that they found a plain in the land of Shinar; and they dwelt there. ³And they said one to another, Go to, let us make brick, and burn them thoroughly. And they had brick for stone, and slime had they for morter. ⁴And they said, Go to, **let us** build us a city and a tower, whose top may reach unto heaven; and ***let us make us a name***, lest we be scattered abroad upon the face of the whole earth. ⁵And the LORD came down to see the city and the tower, which the children of men builded. ⁶And the LORD said, Behold, the people is one, and they have all one language; and this they begin to do: and now nothing will be restrained from them, which they have imagined to do. ⁷Go to, let us go down, and there confound their language, that they may not understand one another's speech. ⁸So the LORD scattered them abroad from thence upon the face of all the earth: and they left off to build the city. ⁹Therefore is the name of it called Babel; because the LORD did there confound the language of all the earth: and from thence did the LORD scatter them abroad upon the face of all the earth.

<u>*Beginning of the Israelite Nation:*</u> (The Committee recognized the continual development of their plan as the following had happened as planned.) The development of

the nation of Israel was to help indicate to mankind through prophecy that (among other things) the Committee could care for a nation and predict ahead of time how events would play out. The record was to be contained in the written Word ahead of time and then verified when the events happened. When mankind saw the events happen AFTER events had been prophesied, the Committee thought and depended on mankind recognizing the Committee and the Committee's abilities. The Committee now began to consider how this event to create Israel as a nation had been recorded and had been carried out. They looked at Genesis 12:1-5 where the development of the nation had been prophesied and in Genesis 15 where the Abrahamic covenant had been made strictly between the members of the Committee. This was considered by the Committee to be an unconditional covenant since mankind was not actually involved in verification of the covenant. The procedure of confirming the covenant has remained hidden by most mankind but the procedure is recorded in the Word for mankind to recognize.

**_Shadows of the first Covenant to Abraham:_** As indicated in the previous discussion of structuring the development of the nation of Israel, Abraham was given some promises that was presented by the Committee and continue to be true. Being a promise from the agreement of the Committee these promises formed the first Covenant as indicated in the Bible recordings. The covenant had three major parts. The descendants of Abraham would be blessed, the land to be given to the nation of Israel was presented, and the people of the entire set of nations would be blessed. This Abrahamic covenant provided results that the nation of Israel was and is promised. Hidden in this covenant was the method in which these three promises would happen. The Committee noted that the land promised to Israel is being a center of conflict today because mankind has not recognized what is intended for Israel in the future. The land will be Israel's as intended. *The warning for mankind is that the Committee will bless those who bless Israel and curse those that curse Israel.* This warning is a truth. The recognition of the fulfillment of the promises comes as a two-fold shadow. One of the shadows that has been accomplished is that Jesus came from Israel and in Him all the people of the entire set of nations can be blessed. However, the truth of the blessing promised is dependent on the acceptance of Jesus as the Messiah through belief. Note in particular the "you" is Abraham and he represents the Israelite nation. Hence, the prediction reaches into the end times when families of the earth will be blessed through Israel. The Committee noted that the Israelite nation has not blessed the families of the earth yet but will in the future. The Committee considered the prophesy of Zechariah recorded in the Word and considered how long "longsuffering" should be determined till . . .

> Genesis 12:1-5 kjv 12 Now the LORD had said unto Abram, Get thee out of thy country, and from thy kindred, and from thy father's house, unto a land that I will shew thee: 2 And I will make of thee a great nation, and I will bless thee, and make thy name great; and thou shalt be a blessing: 3 And I will bless them that bless thee, and curse him that curseth thee: and in

thee shall all families of the earth be blessed. ⁴So Abram departed, as the LORD had spoken unto him; and Lot went with him: and Abram was seventy and five years old when he departed out of Haran. ⁵And Abram took Sarai his wife, and Lot his brother's son, and all their substance that they had gathered, and the souls that they had gotten in Haran; and they went forth to go into the land of Canaan; and into the land of Canaan they came.

The Committee discussed why Abraham (Abram's name was changed.) was to move. As recorded later in the Word for mankind to understand, the use of idols and worship of other gods was already underway in Abraham's original place of abode.

Joshua 24:1-2 kjv ¹And Joshua gathered all the tribes of Israel to Shechem, and called for the elders of Israel, and for their heads, and for their judges, and for their officers; and they presented themselves before God. ²And Joshua said unto all the people, thus saith the LORD God of Israel, Your fathers dwelt on the other side of the flood in old time, even Terah, the father of Abraham, and the father of Nachor: *and they served other gods.*

The Committee discussed mankind and the tendency to worship a god. The opposition's (Satan's and his demons') use of mankind's fleshy body tabernacle and its limitations along with the free will of mankind to make decisions was a major part of plans made. The use of mankind seeing and being tempted by sight was part of a powerful plan of Satan. The plan included the building of idols that could be seen even though mankind should realize that the images were inferior to the creator just as the Creator of the image (mankind) was superior to the creation (mankind and other creation), This plan of Satan as often happened in the plan of the Committee became a part of the great plan of the Committee to show the unseen realm of the spiritual (unseen) so that mankind would accept the Committee as the truth of reality. The Committee recognized this powerful persuasion tactic of Satan and the temptation provided to mankind. The Committee's foreknowledge was again discussed as planning ahead to the time the nation of Israel would want a king and how the Committee had created the plan to have the Messiah be born in the lineage (King David and his lineage) now known by mankind to be the Davidic Covenant. Mankind would accept a king they could see but their true king was unseen until a special prepared body (tabernacle) was recognized as king. The virgin body was discussed as having already come and Israel had trouble understanding and still does. This transition between the seen and the unseen continues to be a problem for mankind. The Committee's plan is for mankind to rely on faith to understand. The Committee discussed their plan to provide mankind substance and evidence for faith in the transition between the seen and the unseen. Again, the Committee was pleased with their plan in support of mankind understanding this difference and accepting through faith by hearing of the Word either verbally or simply through observing natural creations. They recognized the rightful symbolisms including natural examples such as the life cycle of the butterfly becoming a major part of spanning from sight of mankind (seeing) into understanding the possibility of the unseen where the transition was possible (The change of a body (mankind's) into the glorified body as Jesus now had).

In summary: Three important events of the future remain promised in this original covenant to Abram (Abraham). 1. The land is to be provided, 2. The nation (that became Israel) is be considered to be great along with Abraham, 3. The nation is protected by the Committee and any nation (or person) that blesses Israel is blessed and any nation (or person) that curses Israel is cursed. The Committee discussed this permanent covenant and mankind's little observing of who owned the land provided to Israel and described in the Word. Also, little attention is being paid to the warning of the blessing or the curse for nations. Mankind seems to pay little attention of how nations that had not blessed Israel had been cursed throughout history beginning with Egypt, then Assyria and Babylon, and later Germany. The Committee observed the prophesy continues today regardless if mankind pays attention or not.

The sealing of the covenant for confirmation was now considered as provided for mankind in Genesis 15. The promised land for Israel represented a more detailed shadow to understand. The oath was sealed unconditional and not to be broken forever because it was between the Communicator and the rest of the Committee (Careful reading of the Word is needed.). Abram had believed but was asleep during the oath being confirmed which made the covenant unconditionally true. Mankind was known to often break conditional oaths. As time progressed mankind's word had become conditional based on circumstances. Mankind's word changed as circumstances changed. The Committee's Word did not change with time. Methods to achieve the Word did change as needed to promote the true truth. This first covenant could not be broken and provided for the specific destiny for the nation of Israel (the apple of the Committee's eye as recorded in the Word). The shadow pattern for understanding the special position of the nation of Israel was developed through the ages for mankind to recognize. The following excerpt indicates the confirmation established and recorded in the Word. (The Committee noted that the specific land was promised to the Israelite nation from before the nation existed and the confirmation was an unconditional promise sealed by three witnesses (the Committee) as being true with the strongest unbreakable vow . . . The majority of the other nations did not in the present time recognize the future land ownership as promised by the Committee. This failure was to be a major downfall of mankind as in the days of Noah . . . another shadow to be discussed.) The Committee noted that in the Word chapter 15 of Genesis stated the establishment of this covenant and the Egyptian exodus was told ahead of time so that when it happened mankind should see, understand, and believe. (John 14:29 kjv)

> Genesis 15: 12-21 kjv 12 And when the sun was going down, a deep sleep fell upon Abram; and, lo, an horror of great darkness fell upon him. 13 And he said unto Abram, Know of a surety that thy seed shall be a stranger in a land that is not theirs, and shall serve them; and they shall afflict them *four hundred*

*years*; ¹⁴And also that *nation, whom they shall serve, will I judge:* and afterward shall they come out with great substance. ¹⁵And thou shalt go to thy fathers in peace; thou shalt be buried in a good old age. ¹⁶But in the fourth generation they shall come hither again: for the iniquity of the Amorites is not yet full. ¹⁷And it came to pass, that, when the sun went down, and it was dark, behold a smoking furnace, and a burning lamp that passed between those pieces. ¹⁸In the same day the LORD made a covenant with Abram, saying, Unto thy seed have I given this land, from the river of Egypt unto the great river, the river Euphrates: ¹⁹The Kenites, and the Kenizzites, and the Kadmonites, ²⁰And the Hittites, and the Perizzites, and the Rephaims, ²¹And the Amorites, and the Canaanites, and the Girgashites, and the Jebusites.

The Committee noted that the *prophecy of four hundred years* had been fulfilled through the planned development of the Israelite nation and was followed by thirty years till the law was given to Moses. The coming out of Egypt with great substance included the materials to build the tabernacle and its furnishings for worship as planned in the future. This again *was fulfilled and* "fit" into the Committee's plans showing the use of foreknowledge. The setting for this to happen came about through seemingly strange circumstances as time passed . . . again showing the foreknowledge of the Committee. This event had happened. The recorded event was in the written Word for mankind to gain knowledge about the Committee in *using the seen (as mankind needed) to see the unseen* in the mind's eye of mankind through believing (faith) by hearing of the Word (either individually through reading and seeing through their mind's eyes or actually individual hearing of the Word . . . believing and faith was an individual free will decision as evidenced by the determination of Daniel (Daniel 1:8 kjv).

> Exodus 12:40-45 kjv 40 Now the sojourning of the children of Israel, who dwelt in Egypt, was four hundred and thirty years. 41 And it came to pass at the end of the four hundred and thirty years, even the selfsame day it came to pass, that all the hosts of the LORD went out from the land of Egypt. 42 It is a night to be much observed unto the LORD for bringing them out from the land of Egypt: this is that night of the LORD to be observed of all the children of Israel in their generations. 43 And the LORD said unto Moses and Aaron, This is the ordinance of the passover: There shall no stranger eat thereof: 44 But every man's servant that is bought for money, when thou hast circumcised him, then shall he eat thereof. 5 A foreigner and a hired servant shall not eat thereof.

> Daniel 1:8 kjv 8 But Daniel purposed in his heart that he would not defile himself with the portion of the king's meat, nor with the wine which he drank: therefore, he requested of the prince of the eunuchs that he might not defile himself.

The Committee noted not only the fulfillment of the prophesied four hundred years but also the addition of thirty years till the law was given to Moses. Also, the inclusion of the shadow of Jesus as the lamb in the Passover feast was discussed. The Committee also discussed the use of the passover being the lamb itself. The activities set up was to preview Jesus and His destined truth. The shadows continued to be set as Jesus fulfilled in His earthly presentation through teaching and His actual life activities. (Mankind has the saying that "Seeing is believing" as one of their often repeated phrases.) Jesus often used parables that mankind could see in the individual mind's eye to teach with. One of these is the use of a vine to become a shadow of the unseen.

> John 15:1-6 kjv 1 **I** am the true vine, and my Father is the husbandman. 2 Every branch in me that beareth not fruit he taketh away: and every branch that beareth fruit, he purgeth it, that it may bring forth more fruit. 3 Now ye are clean through the word which I have spoken unto you. 4 Abide in me, and I in you. As the branch cannot bear fruit of itself, except it abide in the vine; no more can ye, except ye abide in me. 5 I am the vine, ye are the branches: He that abideth in me, and I in him, the same bringeth forth much fruit: for without me ye can do nothing. 6 If a man abide not in me, he is cast forth as a branch, and is withered; and men gather them, and cast them into the fire, and they are burned.

The Committee noted that the shadows provided by Jesus in the earthly ministry followed the Committee's plan to use the seen (for mankind to see in the mind's eye of experience) to bridge the gap between the seen and the unseen realm of the Committee's existences. Mankind's understanding of the unseen was noted to be from experience of the unseen through shadows. Also, prophesy continued to tell events ahead of time so when they happened, mankind should believe.

The Committee noted that mankind had even adopted a similar plan in their ability to understand the more abstract. In teaching abstract mathematics (mankind planned to see the unseen using shadows and models much as the Committee planned use of shadows and models through time but not recognized by most of mankind). ***It was not recognized by mankind but their plan to understand the abstract was a hidden shadow of the Committee's plan!! Other analogies were patterned by mankind (and continue to be) after the Committee's plan. Afterall, mankind was created in the image of the Committee.***

The Committee noted that some of the promises made by the original covenant of Abraham are still continuing through time and was still being developed even though in general mankind continues to not seem to pay attention to the ongoing fulfillment of the Committee's past, current, and future attention to fulfillment of the promises. The Committee now focused on the use of dreams to reveal prophesied events to mankind. They looked at the dreams of Joseph in their showing of foreknowledge in how the development of care during the four hundred years in the land (now known to be Egypt) would happen due to a famine.

The Committee noted that Abram's grandson Jacob (later to have his name changed to Israel) had twelve sons (one of them being Joseph). These sons were to be the heads of twelve tribes to become the nation of Israel. The dreams given through Joseph were recorded again in the Word for mankind to know.

The Committee continued to look at significant clues related to their foreknowledge. Dreams within the life of Joseph had been used to continue the plan to provide a better foundation for mankind to recognize the ability of the Committee to plan the future. <u>The major goal was that when it comes to pass mankind should come to believe in the unseen spiritual realm and begin to be ready for the mystery to be unveiled later.</u> They had given two dreams to Joseph which were easy to interpret by the family of Joseph at the time but to be fulfilled in an unseen way in the future of the family (recorded for all readers of the Word to understand). The first dream indicated that Joseph would be in a position with his eleven brothers bowing to him. This dream did two things when it was told to his brothers. First, the dream immediately made his brothers to hate him and set in motion a movement that would ultimately set the stage to put Joseph in the position so that the brothers would bow to him. A second unseen result was the unseen care of the creation of the nation of Israel during the prophesied four hundred years in Egypt. The second dream seemed to have a similar message.

> Genesis 37: 5-10 kjv 5 And Joseph dreamed a dream, and he told it his brethren: and they hated him yet the more. 6 And he said unto them, Hear, I pray you, this

dream which I have dreamed: For, behold, we were binding sheaves in the field, and, lo, my sheaf arose, and also stood upright; and, behold, your sheaves stood round about, and made obeisance to my sheaf. ⁸ And his brethren said to him, Shalt thou indeed reign over us? or shalt thou indeed have dominion over us? And they hated him yet the more for his dreams, and for his words. ⁹ And he dreamed yet another dream, and told it his brethren, and said, Behold, I have dreamed a dream more; and, behold, the sun and the moon and the eleven stars made obeisance to me. ¹⁰ And he told it to his father, and to his brethren: and his father rebuked him, and said unto him, What is this dream that thou hast dreamed? Shall I and thy mother and thy brethren indeed come to bow down ourselves to thee to the earth?

Both dreams were fulfilled for mankind to recognize the foreknowledge of the Committee. Through foreknowledge of the Committee, the circumstances in Joseph's life as planned placed Joseph in a command position within Egypt (to be found in the reading of the Word by mankind in the future). The Word preserved the clues for mankind in the future to study and recognize the foreknowledge of the Committee. The recognition by the family of Joseph during the development of the nation is also evident in the Word. Although not discussed by the Committee in detail, the Committee mentioned that the hidden shadow of Joseph's life had been revealed to some of mankind who had explained the shadow as being a physical representation of many attributes of Jesus and the

Committee's overall plan. *The Committee had pleasure in many presentations of the hidden shadows that had now been presented by the plan to bridge the seen-unseen gap. However, the Committee also recognized that Satan had now used a reverse tactic to mislead. Mankind was now needing to divide the truth correctly as indicated in Timothy. The Committee realized that dividing the truth had a two-fold meaning. The dividing of the truth was to divide the truth from the truth, but it was also to divide the truth from the untruth.* Thus the free will choice was needed and the Committee's plan was and continues to provide a foundation for each of mankind (both male and female when coming into the age of accountability to make both decisions of one's own individual free will. The Committee had provided through foreknowledge for mankind that had not come into the age of accountability to be under the Committee's mercy. Mercy was an attribute being revealed to mankind along with the understanding of the mystery that had now been revealed.

The Committee also noted the symbolism and how it was used for a clue to interpret the Word about events not happened yet. They briefly discussed the hidden symbolism in Revelations 12 and decided to discuss the meaning of Revelation 12 in more detail later. They knew a greater meaning would be revealed throughout time as the connection of symbolism began to form a thread throughout the Word (Bible).

(The Committee briefly considered the different versions of the Word created by mankind and noted that the free will often seemed to conflict with the Committee's inspired guidance. The free will of mankind in changing the wording of the Word had also changed some important clues hidden by the original wording in the Word. This was a problem, but they had noted the free will of mankind to continue to be under the control of mankind's determination as planned. The Committee was seeking for mankind to determine as Daniel (and others in recorded summary of Hebrews 11) had done as recorded in Daniel 1:8 and discussed previously. They noted that it was important for mankind to select a good translation of the Word. They quickly noted that mankind seemed to think the wording was easier to understand but the clues were often lost in the translations.)

The circumstances leading to the Committee's planned care and development of Israel had been recorded in the Word and mankind was free (so far) to read and understand about the Committee and the spiritual realm as set out by the Committee. The Committee continued to fulfill the development of the nation of Israel by providing plagues to prompt Egypt to allow the exodus of the developing nation of Israel. They noted the plagues through the guidance of Moses to provide for the exodus but also some hidden meaning in the plagues were left for discussion later. (The Committee noted that time was needed for many of the clue shadows to develop for a greater meaning of truth.) The plagues with some hidden meanings were to be discussed later but for now the recording of the exodus was noted. (Also noted by the Committee was the difference in mankind understanding in a present time and for mankind in a later time. The Committee understood that later mankind within a present time would have a better developed foundation to support a better understanding. The opportunity would be better for understanding provided mankind would determine using individual free will to better understand.

Exodus 12:37-51 kjv ³⁷And the children of Israel journeyed from Rameses to Succoth, about six hundred thousand on foot that were men, beside children. ³⁸And a mixed multitude went up also with them; and flocks, and herds, even very much cattle. ³⁹And they <u>baked unleavened cakes of the dough which they brought forth out of Egypt, for it was not leavened; because they were thrust out of Egypt, and could not tarry, neither had they prepared for themselves any victual</u>. ⁴⁰Now the sojourning of the children of Israel, who dwelt in Egypt, was <u>four hundred and thirty years.</u> ⁴¹And it came to pass at the end of the four hundred and thirty years, even the selfsame day it came to pass, that all the hosts of the LORD went out from the land of Egypt. ⁴²It is a night to be much observed unto the LORD for bringing them out from the land of Egypt: this is that night of the LORD to be observed of all the children of Israel in their generations. ⁴³And the LORD said unto Moses and Aaron, This is the ordinance of the passover: There shall no stranger eat thereof ⁴⁴But every man's servant that is bought for money, when thou hast circumcised him, then shall he eat thereof. ⁴⁵A foreigner and a hired servant shall not eat thereof. ⁴⁶In one house shall it be eaten; thou shalt not carry forth ought of the flesh abroad out of the house;

> *neither shall ye break a bone thereof.* ⁴⁷All the congregation of Israel shall keep it. ⁴⁸And when a stranger shall sojourn with thee, and will keep the passover to the LORD, let all his males be circumcised, and then let him come near and keep it; and he shall be as one that is born in the land: for no uncircumcised person shall eat thereof. ⁴⁹*One law shall be to him that is homeborn, and unto the stranger that sojourneth among you.* ⁵⁰Thus did all the children of Israel; as the LORD commanded Moses and Aaron, so did they. ⁵¹And it came to pass the selfsame day, that the LORD did bring the children of Israel out of the land of Egypt by their armies.

The Committee again noted the hidden shadow of leaving the land of Egypt and journey toward the promised land. This journey as a shadow had been noted by some mankind through inspiration of the comforter that now had come. *However, some of the hidden Word was still to be noted as the journey was made with unleavened bread.* In an extension of this shadow, Jesus had indicated He was the bread of life and He had hidden that He was unleavened as mankind had come to recognize that unleavened was a shadow of a life without sin. The Committee had a continued desire for mankind to bridge the gap between the shadows and believe the true result as in the difference between the shadow of a tree and the tree itself. They had determined when the real body as unleavened bread came in due time that mankind would begin to and surely understand the true representing of the shadow.

<sup>John 6::35 kjv 35</sup>And Jesus said unto them, I am the **bread** of life: he that cometh to me shall never hunger; and he that believeth on me shall never thirst.

Thus, the planned sequence throughout time continued to be as the Committee had planned it. Mankind was to be responsible to individually respond to the Word and the revealing of the Committee's existence and relationship to mankind as intended. The nation of Israel was now beginning to also be the responsibility of the inhabitants and determined by the citizens' free will along with selected leaders. The Committee continued to consider and select some leaders, but the *final decision continues to be resulting from the determination of the free will individual decisions and resulting with the majority national decision.*

The Committee noted that the nation of Israel was still under the unconditional covenant but also noted that the obedience to the covenant by belief as contributed to Abraham's covering of righteousness was an individual condition for each Israelite. The care of the nation was different from the desired individual relationship to the Committee. The future prophecy for the nation of Israel was to show the Israelite and gentile the characteristics of the Committee and their expectations of individual mankind as time proceeded.

The nation is now headed toward the promised land with their journey and entrance to the promised land fulfilling a part of the fulfillment of the covenant. The journey included many circumstances relating the Committee and the Israelite nation (to individuals as to the nation).

These instances happened for mankind's learning and were recorded with mankind being responsible for knowing them. Through inspiration provided mankind was often reminded in the Word either directly or indirectly (through the shadows) of this opportunity.

> Romans 15:4 kjv 4For whatsoever things were written aforetime were written for our learning, that we through patience and comfort of the scriptures might have hope.

The Committee discussed how the directions to Abraham had been to leave his native land because of the worship of idols and other gods in the native land. However, the Committee noted that mankind continued to eyeball surrounding countries and what other nations had. Surrounding countries had kings, so the Israelite nation began to demand a king. The Committee knew that mankind would continue to reject the position of the Committee in relation to mankind. Through foreknowledge again, the Committee had developed plans for kings of Israel and the sequence of events to come. These events were again to be discussed later. However, again the Committee had recorded the decisions of mankind in the Word along with the response of the Committee.

> I Samuel 8: 4-22 kjv 4Then all the elders of Israel gathered themselves together, and came to Samuel unto Ramah, 5And said unto him, Behold, thou art old, and thy sons walk not in thy ways: now *make us a king to judge us like all the nations*. 6But the thing displeased Samuel, when they said, Give us a king

to judge us. And Samuel prayed unto the LORD. ⁷And the LORD said unto Samuel, Hearken unto the voice of the people in all that they say unto thee: *for they have not rejected thee, but they have rejected me, that I should not reign over them.* ⁸*According to all the works which they have done since the day that I brought them up out of Egypt even unto this day, wherewith they have forsaken me, and served other gods, so do they also unto thee.* ⁹Now therefore hearken unto their voice: howbeit yet protest solemnly unto them and shew them the manner of the king that shall reign over them. ¹⁰And Samuel told all the words of the LORD unto the people that asked of him a king. ¹¹And he said, This will be the manner of the king that shall reign over you: He will take your sons, and appoint them for himself, for his chariots, and to be his horsemen; and some shall run before his chariots. ¹²And he will appoint him captains over thousands, and captains over fifties; and will set them to ear his ground, and to reap his harvest, and to make his instruments of war, and instruments of his chariots. ¹³And he will take your daughters to be confectionaries, and to be cooks, and to be bakers. ¹⁴And he will take your fields, and your vineyards, and your oliveyards, even the best of them, and give them to his servants. ¹⁵And he will take the tenth of your seed, and of your vineyards, and give to his officers, and to his servants. ¹⁶And he will take your menservants, and your maidservants, and your goodliest young men, and your asses, and put them to his work. ¹⁷He will take the tenth of your sheep: and ye shall be his servants. ¹⁸And ye shall cry out in that day because of your king which ye shall have chosen you; and the LORD will not hear you in that day. ¹⁹Nevertheless the people refused to obey the voice of Samuel; and they said, Nay; but we will have a king over us; ²⁰That we also may be like all the nations; and that our king may judge us, and go out before us, and fight our battles. ²¹And Samuel heard all the words of the people, and he rehearsed them in the ears of the LORD. ²²And the LORD said to Samuel, Hearken unto their voice, and make them a king. And Samuel said unto the men of Israel, Go ye every man unto his city.

This led to the selection of David as a favored king of Israel and the far-reaching plan that provided another shadow of the planned future by the Committee. David was considered (as was the life of Joseph) to be representative of the planned king of the Kingdom to come. The Committee noted that the thread of symbolism and prophecy had been partially fulfilled but was being set up for a larger truth to come as time proceeded and mankind had the opportunity to have a greater understanding. Historical events continued to fill up the prophesies for mankind to begin to better develop the spiritual realm's existence and the truth (true relationship between the Committee and mankind).
As a result of the continued rejection of the Committee, recorded history in the Word revealed the final split of the nation of Israel into a northern nation known as Israel

(consisting of ten tribes) and a southern nation known as Judea (consisting of two tribes, Juda and Benjamin).

The northern ten tribes were conquered by Assyria and the southern area (Judea) was taken captive by Babylon.

Two important prophesies became evident through Jeremiah. One was the evidence of a change in the basics for the first covenant (although the covenant promises remained in effect). The Committee noted this second covenant was for Israel and designed for the seventieth week of Daniel's prophesy to be discussed later. The Committee discussed the importance of the unconditional promises to Abraham and the conditional agreements between mankind and the Committee. This was stated in the Word as follows as the covenant being broken in the Word below is not the Abrahamic covenant but a later covenant.

> 2nd Covenant: Jeremiah 31:31-32 kjv ³¹Behold, the days come, saith the LORD, that I will make a new covenant with the house of Israel, and with the house of Judah: ³²Not according to the covenant that I made with their fathers in the day that I took them by the hand to bring them out of the land of Egypt; which my covenant they brake, although I was an husband unto them, saith the LORD:

The Committee noted again as in many future events written in the Word that the new covenant had now been revealed through the hidden shadow teachings of Jesus and the mystery as seen and taught by Paul. Paul had the privilege of a visual recognition of Jesus in his glorified body on the road to Damascus. The brilliance as in the days of Moses in receiving the law was such that Paul was blinded for a season. (Paul as an Israelite being blinded was also a shadow of Israel being blinded for a season until a future time of the gentiles be fulfilled.)

> Acts 9:1-9 kjv ¹And Saul, yet breathing out threatenings and slaughter against the disciples of the Lord, went unto the high priest, ²And desired of him letters to Damascus to the synagogues, that if he found any of this way, whether they were men or women, he might bring them bound unto Jerusalem. ³And as he journeyed, he came near Damascus: and *suddenly there shined round about him a light from heaven:* ⁴And he fell to the earth, and heard a voice saying unto him, Saul, Saul, why persecutest thou me? ⁵And he said, Who art thou, Lord? And the Lord said, I am Jesus whom thou persecutest: it is hard for thee to kick against the pricks. ⁶And he trembling and astonished said, Lord, what wilt thou have me to do? And the Lord said unto him, Arise, and go into the city, and it shall be told thee what thou must do. ⁷And the men which journeyed with him stood speechless, hearing a voice, but seeing no man. ⁸And Saul arose from the earth; and when his eyes were opened, he saw no man: but they led him by the hand and brought him into Damascus. ⁹And he was three days without sight, and neither did eat nor drink.

Also, of importance currently was the continued foreknowledge noted by the Committee. This foreknowledge was used in providing mankind an opportunity to see the Committee's ability in planning of future events. The intent continued to be to provide mankind evidence so that when foretold historical events happened mankind would develop a belief in the Committee. Belief in the Committee as Abraham and others had achieved had always been counted as righteousness in place of mankind's sinful nature. For mankind to recognize the righteousness had nothing to do with the later law given by the Committee to Moses by the Messiah in His holiness. Simple belief by Abraham (before the law) was counted for his righteousness as was recorded in the Word.

> <sub>Genesis 15:6 kjv</sub> 6And he believed in the LORD; and he counted it to him for righteousness.

An important prophecy of Jeremiah was the historical prophesy including how long the Israelites would be in captivity to Babylon before Babylon would fall. (Note the original covenant to Abraham had set the condition that a nation that cursed Israel would also be cursed. The Committee continued the truth of this curse (although current nations failed to understand and believe this curse) so Babylon was defeated). The duration that Israel would be held captive was seventy years according to the prophesy of Jeremiah. The reason for the time of seventy years was because the Israelites had failed for four hundred ninety years to set aside the land one year in each seven as stated in the Word as a year of rest for the land. Therefore, the land of Israel was to be vacated for seventy years before the Israelite tribes were permitted to return to their promised land. All this was recorded in the Word for mankind to know and understand.

> <sub>Leviticus 25:1-4 kjv</sub> ¹And the LORD spake unto Moses in mount Sinai, saying, ²Speak unto the children of Israel, and say unto them, When ye come into the land which I give you, then shall the land keep a sabbath unto the LORD. ³Six years thou shalt sow thy field, and six years thou shalt prune thy vineyard, and gather in the fruit thereof; ⁴*But in the seventh year shall be a sabbath of rest unto the land, a sabbath for the LORD: thou shalt neither sow thy field, nor prune thy vineyard.*
> <sub>Jeremiah 25: 12 kjv</sub> ¹²And it shall come to pass, *when seventy years are accomplished*, that I will punish the king of Babylon, and that nation, saith the LORD, for their iniquity, and the land of the Chaldeans, and will make it perpetual desolations.
> <sub>Jeremiah 29:10 kjv</sub> ¹⁰For thus saith the LORD, That *after **seventy years** be accomplished at Babylon I will visit you, and perform my good word toward you, in causing you to return to this place.*

Hence, the 490 years prior to being placed in Babylonian captivity, the Israelite nation had failed to provide the seventh year of rest. The land was due seventy years of rest that had been missed so the Committee had planned a seventy-year rest of the land resulting in a seventy-year captivity of the Israelites away from the land.

The Committee now discussed an excellent prophecy provided through Daniel. This great expression of prophesy through Daniel by planned revelations had now become known by mankind that knew of it as the seventy-week prophecy. (A week of years had been set for Jacob and hidden in the Word several years earlier.)

> Genesis 29:26 kjv 26 And Laban said, It must not be so done in our country, to give the younger before the firstborn. 27 *Fulfill her week*, and we will give thee this also for the service which thou shalt serve with me yet seven other years.

The prophecy given to Daniel had been based on a coming 70-week 490-year period that sixty-nine weeks have now been fulfilled. Daniel was guided to recognize when the end of the Babylonian captivity was completed. This meant that the Committee had revealed a total sequence of 560 years (70 +490) prophecy about Israel to Daniel. (The Committee had kept hidden the mystery time that has now been revealed through Paul's ministry. One week of Daniel's 70-year prophecy is still to follow the revealed mystery age known by mankind as the church age.) This 560-year prophecy should certainly indicate to mankind the foreknowledge of the Committee and provide great evidence to mankind for belief in the Committee as desired. The Committee noted that mankind continues to ignore **evidence and substance** for the basic foundation of appropriate faith. This 490-year prophesy began a great revelation of the history for the nation of Israel as well as other nations in their relation to Israel.

> Daniel 9:2 kjv 2 In the first year of his reign I Daniel understood by books the number of the **years**, whereof the word of the LORD came to Jeremiah

the prophet, that he would accomplish **seventy years** in the desolations of Jerusalem.

<sup>Daniel 9:21-27 kjv</sup> <sup>21</sup>Yea, whiles I was speaking in prayer, even the man Gabriel, whom I had seen in the vision at the beginning, being caused to fly swiftly, touched me about the time of the evening oblation. <sup>22</sup>And he informed me, and talked with me, and said, O Daniel, I am now come forth to give thee skill and understanding. <sup>23</sup>At the beginning of thy supplications the commandment came forth, and I am come to shew thee; for thou art greatly beloved: therefore understand the matter, and consider the vision. <sup>24</sup>Seventy weeks are determined upon thy people and upon thy holy city, to finish the transgression, and to make an end of sins, and to make reconciliation for iniquity, and to bring in everlasting righteousness, and to seal up the vision and prophecy, and to anoint the most Holy. <sup>25</sup>Know therefore and understand, that from the going forth of the commandment to restore and to build Jerusalem unto the Messiah the Prince shall be seven weeks, and threescore and two weeks: the street shall be built again, and the wall, even in troublous times. <sup>26</sup>And after threescore and two weeks shall Messiah be cut off, but not for himself: and the people of the prince that shall come shall destroy the city and the sanctuary; and the end thereof shall be with a flood, and unto the end of the war desolations are determined. <sup>27</sup>And he shall confirm the covenant with many for one week: and in the midst of the

week he shall cause the sacrifice and the oblation to cease, and for the overspreading of abominations he shall make it desolate, even until the consummation, and that determined shall be poured upon the desolate.

(The Committee mentioned briefly about a hidden mystery gap in the Word at this time but decided to discuss this gap later. The gap was the one between the sixty-nine weeks and the seventieth week.)
The Committee had planned on Daniel to be able to interpret some dreams of the Babylonian kings in relation to setting up future nations. These began with a dream by King Nebuchadnezzar that Daniel interpreted. The dream and its interpretation for mankind to read are as follows.

Daniel 2:31-45 kjv 31 Thou, O king, sawest, and behold a great image. This great image, whose brightness was excellent, stood before thee; and the form thereof was terrible. 32 This image's head was of fine gold, his breast and his arms of silver, his belly, and his thighs of brass, 33 His legs of iron, his feet part of iron and part of clay. 34 Thou sawest till that a stone was cut out without hands, which smote the image upon his feet that were of iron and clay and brake them to pieces. 35 Then was the iron, the clay, the brass, the silver, and the gold, broken to pieces together, and became like the chaff of the summer threshing floors; and the wind carried them away, that no place was found for them: and the stone that smote the image became a great mountain, and filled the whole earth. 36 This is the dream; and we will tell the interpretation thereof before the king. ³⁷Thou, O king, art a king of kings: for the God of heaven hath given thee a kingdom, power, and strength, and glory. ³⁸And wheresoever the children of men dwell, the beasts of the field and the fowls of the heaven hath he given into thine hand, and hath made thee ruler over them all. Thou art this head of gold. ³⁹And after thee shall arise another kingdom inferior to thee, and another third kingdom of brass, which shall bear rule over all the earth. ⁴⁰And the fourth kingdom shall be strong as iron: forasmuch as iron breaketh in pieces and subdueth all things: and as iron that breaketh all these, shall it break in pieces and bruise. ⁴¹And whereas thou sawest the feet and toes, part of potters' clay, and part of iron, the kingdom shall be divided; but there shall be in it of the strength of the iron, forasmuch as thou sawest the iron mixed with miry clay. ⁴²And as the toes of the feet were part of iron, and part of clay, so the kingdom shall be partly strong, and partly broken. ⁴³And whereas thou sawest iron mixed with miry clay, they shall mingle themselves with the seed of men: but they shall not cleave one to another, even as iron is not mixed with clay. ⁴⁴And in the days of these kings shall the God of heaven set up a kingdom, which shall never be destroyed: and the kingdom shall not be left to other people, but it shall break in pieces and consume all these kingdoms, and it shall stand for ever. ⁴⁵Forasmuch as thou sawest that the stone was cut out of the mountain without hands, and that it brake in pieces the iron, the brass, the clay, the silver, and the gold; the great God hath made known to the king what shall come to pass hereafter: and the dream is certain, and the interpretation thereof sure.

The Committee recognized again the opportunity provided for mankind to see the Committee's ability to show the historical timeline for nations and their related dominance one after the other throughout the time sequence. The Committee's foreknowledge continues to be a major part of their plan to influence mankind to believe in the spiritual realm and the existence of the Committee.

**The Nations:** The Committee considered the plan for the nations again. Often the plan of the Committee was for mankind to be looking for the evidence of future events. They recognized the destiny of the nations as one of the hidden clues. They knew in the future a few of the nations is to be on the side of the Committee when carrying out the historical future in the seventieth week of Daniel's 490-year prophecy. Most of the nations may side with the "antichrist" or the Satanic realm. Free will decisions of national leaders are now continuing to be made as indicated in the recorded Word. The hidden plan is becoming more revealed in the current history as the nation of Great Britain decided between being an individual nation or a part of the union resulting in the European Union. The United States faces a similar problem as will be noted when the Committee considers the current hidden meaning of the future Tower of Babel. The major problem of mankind has always been and continues to be use of free will to have freedoms without responsibility. Many are now considering a global union of nations in contrast to the individual independency of a nation. This global view is also indicated in the decision to be made by nations. The global view of one government of nations is often discussed in terms of the ten toes of Nebuchadnezzar's statue that was destroyed by the Stone. (Some individual nations need to be on the winning side of the Committee's strategy and hidden in the Word.) The winning side is predicted by the Committee in the recorded Word. The winning side is given as a result of the Committee's foreknowledge to be against the antichrist. According to the plan of the Committee, the winning nations are the ones that side with the apple of the Committee's eye. The Committee noted that there would be individual winners within all nations which are those accepting Jesus as the Christ through faith (Hebrews 11: 1-2 kjv). The Committee through the Word being written and lived continues to provide the substance and evidence needed to build on the innate measure of faith.

> Hebrews 11:1-2 kjv 1 Now faith is the substance of things hoped for, the evidence of things not seen. 2 For by it the elders obtained a good report.

Before the fall of Babylon, during the first year of Belshazzar as king of Babylon, Daniel had a dream consisting of visions which he wrote and recorded in chapter 7 of the Word. This dream provided more details in the sequence of historical nations and added to the original revelation of the statue sequence of nations in the dream of King Nebuchadnezzar. The record showed the following symbolism to reveal the additional information.

<sub>Daniel 7:1-28 kjv</sub> 7 In the first year of Belshazzar king of Babylon Daniel had a dream and visions of his head upon his bed: then he wrote the dream and told the sum of the matters. ²Daniel spake and said, I saw in my vision by night, and, behold, the four winds of the heaven strove upon the great sea. ³And four great beasts came up from the sea, diverse one from another. ⁴The first was like a lion and had eagle's wings: I beheld till the wings thereof were plucked, and it was lifted up from the earth, and made stand upon the feet as a man, and a man's heart was given to it. ⁵And behold another beast, a second, like to a bear, and it raised up itself on one side, and it had three ribs in the mouth of it between the teeth of it: and they said thus unto it, Arise, devour much flesh. ⁶After this I beheld, and lo another, like a leopard, which had upon the back of it four wings of a fowl; the beast had also four heads; and dominion was given to it. ⁷After this I saw in the night visions, and behold a fourth beast, dreadful and terrible, and strong exceedingly; and it had great iron teeth: it devoured and brake in pieces, and stamped the residue with the feet of it: and it was diverse from all the beasts that were before it; and it had ten horns. ⁸I considered the horns, and, behold, there came up among them another little horn, before whom there were three of the first horns plucked up by the roots: and, behold, in this horn were eyes

like the eyes of man, and a mouth speaking great things. ⁹I beheld till the thrones were cast down, and the Ancient of days did sit, whose garment was white as snow, and the hair of his head like the pure wool: his throne was like the fiery flame, and his wheels as burning fire. ¹⁰A fiery stream issued and came forth from before him: thousand thousands ministered unto him, and ten thousand times ten thousand stood before him: the judgment was set, and the books were opened. ¹¹I beheld then because of the voice of the great words which the horn spake: I beheld even till the beast was slain, and his body destroyed, and given to the burning flame. ¹²As concerning the rest of the beasts, they had their dominion taken away: yet their lives were prolonged for a season and time. ¹³I saw in the night visions, and, behold, one like the Son of man came with the clouds of heaven, and came to the Ancient of days, and they brought him near before him. ¹⁴And there was given him dominion, and glory, and a kingdom, that all people, nations, and languages, should serve him: his dominion is an everlasting dominion, which shall not pass away, and his kingdom that which shall not be destroyed. ¹⁵I Daniel was grieved in my spirit during my body, and the visions of my head troubled me. ¹⁶I came near unto one of them that stood by and asked him the truth of all this. So, he told me, and made me know the interpretation of the things. ¹⁷These great beasts, which are four, are four kings, which shall arise out of the earth. ¹⁸But the saints of the most high shall take the kingdom, and possess the kingdom forever, even for ever and ever. [19] Then I would know the truth of the fourth beast, which was diverse from all the others, exceeding dreadful, whose teeth were of iron, and his nails of brass; which devoured, brake in pieces, and stamped the residue with his feet; [20] And of the ten horns that were in his head, and of the other which came up, and before whom three fell; even of that horn that had eyes, and a mouth that spake very great things, whose look was more stout than his fellows. [21] I beheld, and the same horn made war with the saints, and prevailed against them; [22] Until the Ancient of days came, and judgment was given to the saints of the most High; and the time came that the saints possessed the kingdom. [23] Thus he said, The fourth beast shall be the fourth kingdom upon earth, which shall be diverse from all kingdoms, and shall devour the whole earth, and shall tread it down, and break it in pieces. [24] And the ten horns out of this kingdom are ten kings that shall arise: and another shall rise after them; and he shall be diverse from the first, and he shall subdue three kings. [25] And he shall speak great words against the most High, and shall wear out the saints of the most High, and think to change times and laws: and they shall be given into his hand until a time and times and the dividing of time. [26] But the judgment shall sit, and they shall take away his dominion, to consume and to destroy it unto the end. [27] And the kingdom and dominion, and the greatness of the kingdom under

> the whole heaven, shall be given to the people of the saints of the most High, whose kingdom is an everlasting kingdom, and all dominions shall serve and obey him. ²⁸Hitherto is the end of the matter. As for me Daniel, my cogitations much troubled me, and my countenance changed in me: but I kept the matter in my heart.

The Committee recognized that the symbolism was designed to attract mankind to study and try to decipher the meaning. This would be a result of mankind realizing the truth of the prophesy being given by the plan. This attraction would also signal the plan of the Committee working in revealing the future before it happened so mankind would believe as desired. (The Committee continued to discuss the hidden mystery of the revelation to become known with the passage of time.) The Committee then looked at the great sequence of historical events that they had revealed through Daniel during the captivity. The following vision was provided in the third year of King Belshazzar and a clearer interpretation was revealed.

> Daniel 8:1-26 kjv ⁸In the third year of the reign of king Belshazzar a vision appeared unto me, even unto me Daniel, after that which appeared unto me at the first. ²And I saw in a vision; and it came to pass, when I saw, that I was at Shushan in the palace, which is in the province of Elam; and I saw in a vision, and I was by the river of Ulai. ³Then I lifted up mine eyes, and saw, and, behold, there stood before the river a ram which had two horns: and the two horns were high; but one was higher

than the other, and the higher came up last. ⁴I saw the ram pushing westward, and northward, and southward; so that no beasts might stand before him, neither was there any that could deliver out of his hand; but he did according to his will, and became great. ⁵And as I was considering, behold, an he goat came from the west on the face of the whole earth, and touched not the ground: and the goat had a notable horn between his eyes. ⁶And he came to the ram that had two horns, which I had seen standing before the river, and ran unto him in the fury of his power. ⁷And I saw him come close unto the ram, and he was moved with choler against him, and smote the ram, and brake his two horns: and there was no power in the ram to stand before him, but he cast him down to the ground, and stamped upon him: and there was none that could deliver the ram out of his hand. ⁸Therefore the he goat waxed very great: and when he was strong, the great horn was broken; and for it came up four notable ones toward the four winds of heaven. ⁹And out of one of them came forth a little horn, which waxed exceeding great, toward the south, and toward the east, and toward the pleasant land. ¹⁰And it waxed great, even to the host of heaven; and it cast down some of the host and of the stars to the ground, and stamped upon them. ¹¹Yea, he magnified himself even to the prince of the host, and by him the daily sacrifice was taken away, and the place of the sanctuary was cast down. ¹²And an host was given him against the daily sacrifice by reason of transgression, and it cast down the truth to the ground; and it practiced, and prospered. ¹³Then I heard one saint speaking, and another saint said unto that certain saint which spake, How long shall be the vision concerning the daily sacrifice, and the transgression of desolation, to give both the sanctuary and the host to be trodden under foot? ¹⁴And he said unto me, Unto two thousand and three hundred days; then shall the sanctuary be cleansed. ¹⁵And it came to pass, when I, even I Daniel, had seen the vision, and sought for the meaning, then, behold, there stood before me as the appearance of a man. ¹⁶And I heard a man's voice between the banks of Ulai, which called, and said, Gabriel, make this man to understand the vision. ¹⁷So he came near where I stood: and when he came, I was afraid, and fell upon my face: but he said unto me, Understand, O son of man: for at the time of the end shall be the vision. ¹⁸Now as he was speaking with me, I was in a deep sleep on my face toward the ground: but he touched me, and set me upright. ¹⁹And he said, Behold, I will make thee know what shall be in the last end of the indignation: for at the time appointed the end shall be. ²⁰The ram which thou sawest having two horns are the kings of Media and Persia. ²¹And the rough goat is the king of Grecia: and the great horn that is between his eyes is the first king. ²²Now that being broken, whereas four stood up for it, four kingdoms shall stand up out of the nation, but not in his power. ²³And in the latter time of their kingdom, when the transgressors are come to the

> full, a king of fierce countenance, and understanding dark sentences, shall stand up. ²⁴And his power shall be mighty, but not by his own power: and he shall destroy wonderfully, and shall prosper, and practice, and shall destroy the mighty and the holy people. ²⁵And through his policy also he shall cause craft to prosper in his hand; and he shall magnify himself in his heart, and by peace shall destroy many: he shall also stand up against the Prince of princes; but he shall be broken without hand. ²⁶And the vision of the evening and the morning which was told is true: wherefore shut thou up the vision; for it shall be for many days.

Babylon fell and the Medes and Persians came into power with the Persians being most powerful with King Darius. Daniel (as Joseph in previous years had been promoted into a position to carry out the plan in developing Israel as a nation when in Egypt) was promoted to third in position within the Persian governing body. This put Daniel in a favored position to carry out the plan as the Committee directed in prophesy. Daniel was given visions that provided revelations concerning the sequence of nations. The Committee now began to look at the great sequence of nations resulting in the completed history of nations and the change of the focus of prophesy into the second phase of dividing the truth for understanding. The final prophesy involved a change of focus although other prophets included some added detail to be discussed as time permitted in the Committee's current meeting.

The prophesy to become known by mankind as the seventy weeks of years prophesy came about due to Daniel asking about the seventy-year captivity that Jeremiah prophesied being over. Note that Daniel believed in the prophesy as the Committee desired for all mankind. The recorded Word is as follows.

> Daniel 9:1-2 kjv ¹In the first year of Darius the son of Ahasuerus, of the seed of the Medes, which was made king over the realm of the Chaldeans; ²In the first year of his reign I Daniel understood by books the number of the years, whereof the word of the LORD came to Jeremiah the prophet, that he would accomplish seventy years in the desolations of Jerusalem.

The seventy-week (490-year) prophesy was revealed to Daniel and hidden to some respect due to the use of time to actually provide a deeper understanding. Hidden in this sequential history of nations was a focus on Israel and the Committee's continued fulfillment of the original Abrahamic covenant. The Committee was careful to indicate to Daniel that the seventy weeks was determined on "thy" people which would be the Israelites to often be designated simply as the Jews. (Although the entire nation of twelve tribes was to be considered.)

The Committee had designated Gabriel to carry this message to Daniel. The message of seventy weeks was presented in chapter 9 of Daniel in the Word and preserved for mankind to understand at least partially as shown in history and as the Committee has already discussed.

**More than a Shadow: <u>The Seventy Weeks of Years</u>** . . . A hidden revealing of the ability of the Committee to see into the future was to show an abundant use of their foreknowledge attribute. To show more directly this attribute was planned in what has now become known by mankind as the seventy-week historical sequence revealed to Daniel and then recorded. One needs to understand that the week is a week of years or seven years. The Committee planned to provide clues that the week was a week of seven years as provided in another recording based on Jacob serving for a week of years in order to get Rachel for his wife. Thus, mankind had now come to recognize the seventy weeks covered four hundred ninety years of history for mankind to gradually see unfold as time passed. (One of the major events within this prophecy was the freely given death of the lamb on the cross. The timing of the cross had been revealed in the 69-week prophecy.) The Committee noted that it was during Daniel's special prayer on behalf of Israel and recorded in the Word that the great 70-week prophecy was revealed.

> Daniel 9:3-20 kjv 3And I set my face unto the Lord God, to seek by prayer and supplications, with fasting, and sackcloth, and ashes: 4And I prayed unto the LORD my God, and made my confession, and said, O Lord, the great and dreadful God, keeping the covenant and mercy to them that love him, and to them that keep his commandments; 5*We* have sinned, and have committed iniquity, and have done wickedly, and have rebelled, even by departing from thy precepts and from thy

judgments: ⁶Neither have _we_ hearkened unto thy servants the prophets, which spake in thy name to _our_ kings, _our_ princes, and _our_ fathers, and to _all the people_ of the land. ⁷O LORD, righteousness belongeth unto thee, but unto _us_ confusion of faces, as at this day; to the men of Judah, and to the inhabitants of Jerusalem, and unto _all Israel_, that are near, and that are far off, through all the countries whither thou hast driven _them_, because of their trespass that _they_ have trespassed against thee. ⁸O Lord, to _us_ belongeth confusion of face, to _our_ kings, to _our_ princes, and to _our_ fathers, because _we_ have sinned against thee. ⁹To the Lord _our_ God belong mercies and forgivenesses, though _we_ have rebelled against him; ¹⁰Neither have _we_ obeyed the voice of the LORD _our_ God, to walk in his laws, which he set before _us_ by his servants the prophets. ¹¹Yea, _all Israel_ have transgressed thy law, even by departing, that _they_ might not obey thy voice; therefore the curse is poured upon _us_, and the oath that is written in the law of Moses the servant of God, because _we_ have sinned against him. ¹²And he hath confirmed his words, which he spake against _us_, and against _our_ judges that judged _us_, by bringing upon _us_ a great evil: for under the whole heaven hath not been done as hath been done upon Jerusalem. ¹³As it is written in the law of Moses, all this evil is come upon _us_: yet made _we_ not _our_ prayer before the LORD _our_ God, that _we_ might turn from _our_ iniquities, and understand thy truth. ¹⁴Therefore hath the LORD watched upon the evil, and brought it upon _us_: for the LORD _our_ God is righteous in all his works which he doeth: for _we_ obeyed not his voice. ¹⁵And now, O Lord _our_ God, that hast brought thy people forth out of the land of Egypt with a mighty hand, and hast gotten thee renown, as at this day; _we_ have sinned, _we_ have done wickedly. ¹⁶O LORD, according to all thy righteousness, I beseech thee, let thine anger and thy fury be turned away from thy city Jerusalem, thy holy mountain: because for _our_ sins, and for the iniquities of _our_ fathers, Jerusalem and thy people are become a reproach to all that are about _us_. ¹⁷Now therefore, O our God, hear the prayer of thy servant, and his supplications, and cause thy face to shine upon thy sanctuary that is desolate, for the Lord's sake. ¹⁸O my God, incline thine ear, and hear; open thine eyes, and behold _our_ desolations, and the city which is called by thy name: for _we_ do not present our supplications before thee for _our_ righteousnesses, but for thy great mercies. ¹⁹O Lord, hear; O Lord, forgive; O Lord, hearken and do; defer not, for thine own sake, O my God: for thy city and thy people are called by thy name. ²⁰And whiles I was speaking, and praying, and confessing my sin and the sin of my people Israel, and presenting my supplication before the LORD my God for the holy mountain of my God;

(The Committee made a brief note that recently President Trump of the United States had used the term "us" in a telephone message to represent the entire country rather than just himself. This difference in thought was the same as that used by Daniel in his special prayer. For Daniel "us" and "we" meant all of Israel.)

The Committee also noted that the prophecy had a gap of time in it that was to be understood by mankind in the future. The gap existed between the following phrases recorded in the prophecy when the "Messiah be cut off, but not for himself" and "the people of the prince that shall come shall destroy the city and the sanctuary". Mankind of the present time should readily recognize Jesus being crucified and the people of the prince to come being the Roman people based on the destruction of Jerusalem in 70 AD. This destruction of the physical sanctuary commonly referred to as the temple (originally recognized as the tabernacle). This conquering of Jerusalem led to the scattering of the Israelites (commonly just referred to as Jews). The Committee noted the shadow of the tabernacle was carried through in meaning and was substance for understanding.

(The tabernacle and temple had been revealed as representing the body of mankind and recorded in the Word for mankind to recognize. Farther, the Committee commented on the feast of tabernacles in meaning. The disciples learned as time passed and as the Committee hoped mankind would learn from fulfilled prophecy. Learning as intended was also recorded in the Word.)

> John 2:18-22 kjv 18Then answered the Jews and said unto him, What sign shewest thou unto us, seeing that thou doest these things? 19Jesus answered and said unto them, Destroy this temple, and in three days

I will raise it up. ²⁰ Then said the Jews, Forty and six years was this temple in building, and wilt thou rear it up in three days? ²¹ But he spake of the temple of his body. ²² *When therefore he was risen from the dead, his disciples remembered that he had said this unto them; and they believed the scripture, and the word which Jesus had said.*

The above revelation had some symbolism and as time progressed the Committee noted that the focus continued to be on the Israelite nation and the revealing of a planned method to provide a cure for the nature of sin resulting from mankind's lack of being responsible for needed appropriate control of the individual free will. The additional revelation in chapter 9 and 10 of Daniel resulted in symbolism that was to be revealed after Daniel's time and near the end times. Daniel was told to close the vision till the end. Mankind of the future were then and now present are to consider and watch for what is happening with the nations. There is the major clue related to watching the revelation and unfolding of the future of "thy" people (The Israelites). The Committee expected mankind to now know about the use of Israel as a major focus in history past, present, and future. The Committee noted that Israel has become a physical time clock of prophecy if mankind pays attention to understand.

> Daniel 12:4 kjv 4 But thou, O Daniel, shut up the words, and seal the book, even to the time of the end: many shall run to and fro, and knowledge shall be increased.

(The Committee briefly considered that as time passed the truth of many of mankind running to and fro and the rapidity of knowledge increasing through use of technology is in place. They also noted that some prophecies found in the recorded word are becoming possible based on the use of the increased knowledge.)
The Committee noted that time has now passed, and mankind could understand that the future has already unfolded for the first sixty-nine weeks. The messiah has come (Jesus has come.) and been cut off (crucified on the cross) not for himself (providing forgiveness of all mankind's sins if they believed). Also, the people of the prince that shall come indicated fulfillment in the destruction of Jerusalem and the sanctuary seventy years after the virgin birth. (The Committee also commented on the possible meaning in reference to the antichrist in the middle of the seventieth week still to be revealed physically and anticipated by some of mankind.) Many of mankind have now filled in the gaps of history as time began to reveal the end time plan. The Committee also noted that the fulfillment of the seventieth week left Daniel's prophecy to be continued at a time following the death, burial, and resurrection of Jesus and the destruction of the Temple in 70 AD. The "gap of time" being the mystery was to happen (and is currently happening) before the seventieth week.

At the time of Jesus, the Israelites failed to respond to Jesus as the Messiah when He came in a physical body and was not what the Jews (Israelites) expected although a remnant believed. The revelation of clues about who Jesus was to be had been presented within prophesy as had the history of nations. This revelation of Jesus through prophecy is now considered by the Committee as ***the major division*** of the recorded truth to be understood by mankind. The Committee had used the same plan to tell about Jesus ahead of time just as they had told of the sequential time elements of the nations. The Committee noted their continued expectancy for mankind being responsible to accept and believe in Jesus as the promised messiah. Although much more about the nations could be found in the recorded Word the Committee now turned to consider the prophecy of Jesus as provided by the Word.

## Chapter III

### *Truth 2: The Coming of Jesus to Israel as the Messiah*

**_The Foundation for Jesus:_** The Committee now turned to discussing their major plan to support mankind in getting rid of the Adamic sin that was inherited through the mystery of the blood line. This acceptance of Jesus as a substitute for a needed sacrifice with a pure blood line to save all who believed was the central plan of the Committee. The Committee knew of a plan as they had developed ahead of time with foreknowledge. Foreknowledge was used in designing the image of mankind. Man (not woman) was responsible for the offspring being man or female. Through man the blood line was determined. Therefore, a virgin birth had been planned for providing a pure blood line for the second Adam.

The acceptance of Jesus as the Messiah was and is based on Jesus in his physical life fulfilling the provided prophetic revelations that had been preplanned. Many circumstances of His physical life were told ahead of time so when He fulfilled the prophecies mankind (The Jews at the time of His actual physical life) would and will accept Him as the Messiah. Many prophecies had been recorded in the Word that Jesus fulfilled in His physical life with some to still be fulfilled. The Committee discussed a few of these prophecies. The following are the few references discussed as prophesied in the Word to verify that Jesus was the true Messiah. The Jews needed to believe as a final remnant will in the future. Remember that **belief** in the Committee and now in Jesus being the Messiah continues to substitute for righteousness as it did for Abraham and others.

**<u>Shadow in the Garden:</u>** The Garden of Eden and the fall of mankind has already been discussed. The Committee again discussed the often-hidden clue that mankind could not cover the sin but needed a blood sacrifice. This need had been made evident from the garden episode. Adam and Eve had tried to cover up, but the Communicator showed the shadow of the sacrifice needed by providing coats of skins for a covering. From the beginning, shedding of blood was a shadow of the true sacrifice to come. (*<u>The shedding of a pure blood resulting from the virgin birth was needed. This came on the cross.</u>*) The Committee noted this event as one of the early evidences that a sacrifice was needed.

> Genesis 3:7-10 kjv 7And the eyes of them both (Adam and Eve) were opened, and they knew that they were naked; and <u>*they sewed fig leaves together and made themselves aprons*</u>. 8And they heard the voice of the LORD God walking in the garden in the cool of the day: and Adam and his wife hid themselves from the presence of the LORD God amongst the trees of the garden. 9And the LORD God called unto Adam, and said unto him, Where art thou? 10And he said, I heard thy voice in the

garden, and I was afraid, because I was naked; and I hid myself.

<sub>Genesis 3:21 kjv 21</sub>Unto Adam also and to his wife did <u>the LORD God make coats of skins, and clothed them.</u>

(<u>The shedding of a pure blood resulting from the virgin birth was needed. This came on the cross.</u>) The remission of sins depended on the mystery decision by the Committee and depended on the pure sacrificial blood of Jesus from the virgin birth. The Committee had accepted sacrifices of animals accompanied by belief in the Committee prior to the Cross. John the Baptist preached the baptism of repentance for the remission of sins in preparation for Jesus. Jesus came and became the pure sacrifice needed. After the shedding of His blood no other sacrifice was and is to be available. The acceptance of the blood of Jesus resulted in the apostles and the generations after the cross preaching remission of sins through appropriate belief in the name of Jesus.

***Prior to the Cross:*** <sub>Mark 1: 4 kjv 4</sub>John did baptize in the wilderness, and preach the baptism of repentance for the **remission** of sins.

***At the Cross:*** <sub>Matthew 26:28 kjv 28</sub>For this is my blood of the new testament, which is shed for many for the **remission** of sins.

<sub>Romans 3:25 kjv 25</sub>Whom God hath set forth to be a propitiation through faith in his blood, to declare his righteousness for the **remission** of sins that are past, through the forbearance of God;

Hebrews 9:22 kjv ²²And almost all things are by the law purged with blood; and without shedding of blood is no **remission**.

Hebrews 10:18 kjv 18Now where **remission** of these is, there is no more offering for sin

**In His name:** Acts 10:43 kjv 43To him give all the prophets witness, that through his name whosoever believeth in him shall receive **remission** of sins.
*A hidden representation of the Seed to be*. Mankind were and are to follow the seed of woman to solve a huge mystery. (The reason for the needed virgin birth was to not have the continued transfer of sin through the man's bloodline. This is true by belief but a mystery.) This mystery was revealed in the Garden of Eden also as He spoke to the serpent about woman's (not man's) seed.

Genesis 3:15-16 kjv 15And I will put enmity between thee and the woman, and between thy seed and her seed; it shall bruise thy head, and thou shalt bruise his heel. 16Unto the woman he said, I will greatly multiply thy sorrow and thy conception, in sorrow thou shalt bring forth children; and thy desire shall be to thy husband, and he shall rule over thee.

The Committee discussed a serious mistake usually made in mankind's discussion and teaching of the fall in the garden. The focus is usually on Eve being the first to sin. However, the Committee made a distinction on the *cause* of Eve's sin being different from the *cause* of Adam's sin. The Committee noted that the sin of mankind through history and been termed in the Word as the Adamic sin. The difference in the causes was that Eve was tempted in her sin, but Adam's sin was not out of temptation but a decision of his individual free will. The free will of mankind *and* the responsibility for free will individual decisions continue to form an inseparable pair in the eyes of the Committee. Paul noted this in his message.

> I Timothy 2:14 kjv ¹⁴And Adam was not deceived, but the woman being deceived was in the transgression.

**<u>The Birth of Jesus:</u>** <u>Shadow of the Virgin Birth:</u> The prophet Isaiah revealed several characteristics of the physical life of Jesus including that He would be born of a virgin. This event as told through Isaiah has now already happened and is now recognized by many that believe and many that have believed. Many of mankind knew the story by head knowledge but the new covenant expressed through Jeremiah 31:31 included a circumcision that was not a physical circumcision but a knowledge circumcision being heartfelt through belief. The statement provided in the Word is given below. The Committee discussed mankind's recognition of the Committee's plan in changing the symbolism of circumcision from the physical circumcision stated to Abraham through to the cross and then the changing to an inward circumcision symbolism of the heart. For mankind, the understanding of the difference was <u>through the Comforter's entrance to be discussed more in detail later.</u>

Romans 2:29 kjv 29But he is a Jew, which is one inwardly; and circumcision is that of the heart, in the spirit, and not in the letter; whose praise is not of men, but of God.

The Committee again remembered the Word given to Jeremiah in prophesy ahead of time.

Jeremiah 31:31-31 kjv 31Behold, the days come, saith the LORD, that I will make a new covenant with the house of Israel, and with the house of Judah: 32Not according to the covenant that I made with their fathers in the day that I took them by the hand to bring them out of the land of Egypt; which my covenant they brake, although I was an husband unto them, saith the LORD:

*The need for the virgin birth:* As noted, the major transgression of not obeying the commandments of the Committee in the Garden of Eden established the sinful nature of mankind. Note that Eve was the first to be tempted by Satan and did sin. The Committee again recognized that most people think that Eve is the cause of Adam sinning and in a way that is correct, but Satan did not tempt Adam to sin. Adam of his own free will decided to join Eve because of his love for her. In consideration of the second commandment of love Adam broke the commandment of God to not eat of the tree of knowledge of good and evil. In the breaking of this Committee's commandment Adam committed the Adamic sin of his own free will. This made his sin different from Eve's and was considered by the Committee to have contaminated the blood line and this free will sin was inherited within mankind from then on and known as the Adamic sin.

A "pure" blood sacrifice was then demanded by the Committee to satisfy the restoration of "purity" for mankind. Since man was responsible for the blood transference for babies the hidden plan had been to have the virgin birth to provide the "pure" blood sacrifice . . . Jesus on the cross. (The Committee briefly discussed that mankind in science has shown that based on the x or y transference of mankind in reproduction, it is the male that determines the male or female baby.)

> Isaiah 7:14 kjv 14Therefore the Lord himself shall give you a sign; Behold, a virgin shall conceive, and bear a son, and shall call his name Immanuel.

This virgin birth has now been recorded in the Word within the Gospels of Mathew and Luke where the genealogies of both Mary and Joseph have been revealed with both being in the genealogy of King David. The Davidic Covenant was discussed since it has been fulfilled through the woman's (Mary's) seed as indicated in the Garden of Eden.

*The Shadow of The Davidic Covenant:* Another hidden part of the plan involved the representation of the bodily form of Christ as He is to return as king in the final move of victory. The special images (mankind-men and women) that make the free will choice to believe and accept the plan of redemption through the death, burial, and resurrection will be a part of this kingdom (either in governing or otherwise). The body of Jesus was noted as being important in the Committee's discussion. They decided to discuss this as the cross discussion was coming.

For now, the Committee simply mentioned that the body of Jesus (seen) had been presented as a representation of the unseen spiritual realm. The indicated fulfillment of Jesus being descended form David of the Old Testament lies in both the lineage of Mary as Jesus' mother and the husband Joseph. The man could not be the father in the Committee's plan since Adam made the decision to sin of his own free will. Thus, the recorded Word indicates a difference between the first Adam and the second Adam (Jesus). From revelation of this hidden sign comes Jesus forth as the king in a final victory. The Committee noted the genealogies of both Joseph and Mary given in the Word. Joseph came through the lineage of Solomon the son of King David.

> Matthew 1:6-16 kjv 6And Jesse begat David the king; and David the king begat Solomon of her that had been the wife of Urias; . . . 16And Jacob begat Joseph the husband of *Mary, of whom was born Jesus*, who is called Christ.

The Committee noted that the recorded Word did not indicate Joseph as the father, but that Mary was the one "of whom was born Jesus."

Mary came through the lineage of Nathan the son of King David. The Committee again mentioned the care not to indicate Joseph as being the father. Thus, the lineage for the Davidic covenant was continued through Mary and the REAL king to be was Jesus.

> Luke 3: 23-32 jkv 23 And Jesus himself began to be about thirty years of age, being (as was supposed) the son of Joseph, which was the son of Heli, . . . ³¹ Which was the son of Melea, which was the son of Menan, which was the son of Mattatha, which was the son of Nathan, which was the son of David, ³² Which was the son of Jesse, . . .

The importance of Jesus taking on the body of mankind through the virgin birth was indicated in the Word and supported in the following scriptures in Hebrews.

> Hebrews 10:5 kjv 5 Wherefore when he cometh into the world, he saith, Sacrifice and offering thou wouldest not, but a *body* hast thou prepared me:

> Hebrews 10:10 kjv 10 By the which will we are sanctified through the offering of the *body of Jesus Christ once for all*.

The birth of Jesus was foretold ahead of time as occurring in Bethlehem Ephratah. Mankind was to recognize how the Committee worked this out. The methods that the Committee had brought about the fulfillment of the prophesies was to be a learning experience for mankind continuing to establish belief as desired. The Committee used the king of Rome Augustus Caesar to provide fulfillment of the virgin birth happening in Bethlehem as told above 400 years previously in the prophetic Word of Micah. The Committee discussed the fact that there was two Bethlehems and the Word was specific and true that the place of birth was Bethlehem Ephratah.

<sup>Micah 5:2 jkv 2</sup>But thou, Bethlehem Ephratah, though thou be little among the thousands of Judah, yet out of thee shall he come forth unto me that is to be ruler in Israel; whose goings forth have been from of old, from everlasting.

The Committee had set the stage for the virgin birth being in Bethlehem Ephratah through a former Jew named Jesse who lived in Bethlehem Ephratah. Jesse was the father of King David making the lineage of David having a hometown of Bethlehem Ephratah. As a result, Joseph and Mary being in the lineage of David had their hometown as Bethlehem Ephratah. (NOTE: It is important that both Mary and Joseph have the lineage from David in order to fulfill the prophesy of the Word in Micah. (This planning should show mankind the foreknowledge plan preparation by the Committee. Who of the created image could have planned this lineage so it fulfilled the two conditions fulfilled the prophecy of Micah? How could Micah have known? Only through inspired revelation from the Committee.) The two conditions of lineage resulted that Mary was to provide the virgin birth and Joseph needed to go to Bethlehem Ephratah for taxation. The Committee noted this twofold planning result should lead mankind to understand their planning in the fulfillment of the prophesy in Micah.) King Augustus Caesar demanded that all Jews be taxed at their hometown. Therefore, Joseph had to go to Bethlehem Ephratah to be taxed as head of the family. (*Hence, Joseph's lineage to be from King David was important for a different reason than Mary being in the lineage of King David.* Many mankind has missed this need and wondered about the difference in the lineage. Many wondered why the two lineages were given. Hidden was two different clues.) The Committee arranged this sequence in order to fulfill the two different conditions resulting in fulfillment of the virgin birth being in Bethlehem Ephratah-the virgin birth by Mary and the place of birth through Joseph. The Committee was pleased in how they had set this up and hoped that mankind could recognize their planning on details to bring forth the fulfillment of prophecy. Mankind should recognize the wisdom of the Committee is setting up the clues of truth. This sequence was also recorded in the Word, but the sequence was located as one of many clues. The sequence was in Micah and then chasing through the genealogies in Mathew and in Luke as indicated below.

> Luke 2:1-6 kjv 1 And it came to pass in those days, that there went out a decree from Caesar Augustus that all the world should be taxed. 2(And this taxing was first made when Cyrenius was governor of Syria.) 3 And all went to be taxed, everyone into his own city. 4 And Joseph also went up from Galilee, out of the city of Nazareth, into Judaea, unto the city of David, which is called Bethlehem; (because he was of the house and lineage of David:) 5 To be taxed with Mary his espoused wife, being great with child. 6 And so it was, that, while they were there, the days were accomplished that she should be delivered.

The Committee could not help but also mention that a third evidence of the Committee's planning included the action of Augustus Caesar to order the need for taxation at the time needed for fulfillment of the Bethlehem Ephratah prophecy. The Committee also mentioned a fourth evidence that this was during the Israelite feast of tabernacles which resulted in not space for Joseph and Mary to find a place in an inn, so Jesus was born in a manger. Planning by the Committee was deep in comparison to the ability of mankind although the ability of mankind (being created in the image of the Committee) was far above other created live creatures.

***The Physical Life of Jesus:*** The Committee noted that other prophesies related to His birth and childhood had been fulfilled along with definite shadows of His life leading up to the cross. The Committee became more and more pleased with the plan to help mankind recognize the unseen realm as well as to recognize the redemption plan through the sacrifice of a pure blood representative substitute . . . Jesus. Throughout prophesy in the Word mankind had been mystified by the description of the suffering Messiah being the victorious King and priest. The study of symbolism had depicted these characteristics of Jesus as the suffering Messiah that came, His present priesthood, and Him still to come King.

*The Shadow of the Physical Tabernacle:* The Committee's plan of the tabernacle given to Moses contained several future pictures of Jesus as the Messiah. These hidden pictures were revealed by Jesus in His earthly ministry which is recorded in the Word for mankind to recognize. The life of the Messiah had (and now has been) been depicted by the physical building of the tabernacle in Exodus according to the specific detailed directions given to Moses. Mankind has now analyzed the representation of Jesus' life including his teachings. He has represented Himself in fulfillment of the furniture outlined by the Committee for Moses to have built. These included the sacrifice of the lamb offering, the light, the washing, the bread, and the alter of incense in the holy place along with a division curtain between the holy place and the most holy place. Behind the curtain of division after the holy place was the most holy place representing the special dwelling place of God. Special symbols representing Jesus as the fulfillment of the law and prophecy were included in the most holy place. The overall shape of the furniture as placed in the tabernacle from an above view was a cross. The Committee noted that mankind has been inspired to understand most of the hidden symbolism about Jesus within the structure outlined by the tabernacle. The Committee noted that mankind has written several books interpreting the tabernacle and it as a shadow of Jesus as the Christ. Mankind was and is encouraged to study the tabernacle for the hidden shadows of Jesus.

*The fulfillment in the Physical Realm:* The birth was only the beginning of prophetic fulfillment for mankind to see and hopefully believe. The Committee briefly now looked at the beginning of the Communicator in the physical body of Jesus and now noted His ministry in His physical body being specifically to Israel. The ministry of the Communicator member of the Committee as Jesus had been recorded in the Word at least two notable times for mankind to recognize. For mankind living at the time of the cross, prophecy identifying Jesus as the Messiah **had** been presented and for mankind living after the cross more of the prophecy **has** been presented.

The first indication of the mission of Jesus came when He presented scriptures in the synagogue indicating an important phase in the way the clues were given for mankind's interpretation. In the synagogue He indicated his partial fulfillment of the scriptures in the physical life of Jesus as was recorded for mankind to study and learn. The Committee through foreknowledge knew that Jesus had fulfilled the symbol of the lamb for sacrifice and not for the latter time in the future when He would return as a lion for a different task in judgement. Jesus knew this division in time and indicated it in His following teaching. The Committee noted a time gap in the scriptures as a hidden clue. Comparison of the scripture presented by Jesus with lack of finishing the prophesy by Isaiah indicates the time gap not to be fulfilled by Jesus during His physical ministry.

> Luke 4:16-20 kjv 16 And he came to Nazareth, where he had been brought up: and, as his custom was, he went into the synagogue on the sabbath day, and stood up for to read. 17 And there was delivered unto him the book of the prophet Esaias. And when he had opened the book, he found the place where it was written, 18 The Spirit of the Lord is upon me, because he hath anointed me to preach the gospel to the poor; he hath sent me to heal the brokenhearted, to preach deliverance to the captives, and recovering of sight to the blind, to set at liberty them that are bruised, 19 To preach the acceptable year of the Lord. 20 And he closed the

book, and he gave it again to the minister, and sat down. And the eyes of all them that were in the synagogue were fastened on him.

The prophesy actually provided by Isaiah was:

> Isaiah 61: 1 kjv ¹The Spirit of the Lord GOD is upon me; because the LORD hath anointed me to preach good tidings unto the meek; he hath sent me to bind up the brokenhearted, to proclaim liberty to the captives, and the opening of the prison to them that are bound; ²To proclaim the acceptable year of the LORD, **_and the day of vengeance of our God; to comfort all that mourn:_** . . .

The Committee noted that vengeance was still in the future at the present time and would happen in the seventieth week of the prophesy given to Daniel. Gaps in time was a method of hiding clues of prophecy that the Committee noted as being used in the Word.

*The Gap Clues*: The Committee now discussed the use of time gaps in the planned clues. These were often difficult for mankind to recognize. One significant time gap noted that mankind has discussed is the gap of time between the first 69 weeks of Daniel and the seventieth week. Now in His reading Jesus provides another time gap between his physical body timeline as the Lamb and His time of vengeance as the Lion of the tribe of Judah. The Committee noted that this gap between Jesus as the Lamb and Jesus as the Lion and the gap between the 69th week and 70th week of Daniel is the same gap and should be recognized as such by mankind. Of major importance for mankind to recognize is that Jesus indicated this gap when He stopped reading in the middle of a verse and did not complete the verse. The Committee noted that Jesus had not finished the following part of the scripture recorded in the prophecy of Isaiah 61:1-2. Jesus had not finished verse 2 because Jesus knew He was not going to fulfill the latter part of the scripture during His earthly ministry. The Committee recognized that often there were gaps in the clues that mankind had to learn about in interpretation of the clues. This was a part of dividing the Word to discover the division of Truth. They remembered that in Timothy Paul had reminded mankind to correctly divide the Word of Truth. Jesus gave mankind an example for correctly dividing the Word of Truth since in His ministry as Jesus He was not going to fulfill the latter part of verse 2 below. The Committee again noted as an important time gap clue that the day of vengeance referred to the seventieth week of Daniel to come later.

> Isaiah 61:2 kjv 2 To proclaim the acceptable year of the LORD, *and the day of vengeance of our God; to comfort all that mourn;*

A second time that Jesus discussed His ministry was with the disciples. The Committee noted that most mankind had not studied the Word and did not recognize this division of the Word of Truth. This was the important mission of Jesus to come *only to present the Truth to the selected nation of Israel and the Israelites (Jews).* Even though the Committee knew by foreknowledge that the rejection of the Truth was to come from the Jews, the opportunity for the Jews to exercise their free will and accept the plan for a kingdom at the time of Jesus was to be available. (Through foreknowledge the Committee had the plan in place for completion of the pure sacrifice needed.) Jesus expressed His mission as follows and again recorded the mission in the Word for mankind's opportunity to understand the Committee's goal as time revealed more of the ultimate plan's details. A lot of mankind did not realize that Jesus came under the Law of Moses and fulfilled that law perfectly being the only representative of mankind to do so and fulfill the law in a perfect manner as He stated in the Word. Jesus had stated it this way as recorded in the Word.

> Matthew 5:17 kjv 17Think not that I am come to destroy the law, or the prophets: I am not come to destroy, but to fulfil.

Jesus limited his ministry to Israel (and only went to mankind outside of Israel based on individual belief in the Committee). He also limited his apostles in the same manner. (This limitation was to be on the apostles for the duration of their life amounting to an important division between the prophecies indicated in the Word and the mystery to come. The Committee noted that later the apostles would minster to Israel while Paul would minister to the gentiles in particular.) One of the instances recorded in the Word of gentile belief making a difference is recorded in the Word when a gentile woman came to Jesus. He at first refused her request.

<sup>Matthew 15:23-24 kjv 23</sup>But he answered her not a word. And his disciples came and besought him, saying, Send her away; for she crieth after us. ²⁴But he answered and said, *I am not sent but unto the lost sheep of the house of Israel.*

The disciples had been limited in the word as follows. In the Word was recorded the message and directions for the twelve to go only to the "lost sheep" of Israel.

<sup>Matthew 15:5-6 kjv</sup> ⁵These twelve Jesus sent forth, and commanded them, saying, Go not into the way of the Gentiles, and into any city of the Samaritans enter ye not: ⁶But go rather to the lost sheep of the house of Israel.

This limitation to the apostles *was followed even after the cross and was to be discussed as the Committee discussed the transition following the cross*. The Committee noted a hidden clue related to the mystery to be revealed later given by Jesus as follows: The Committee remembered that the tribes of Israel were to be scattered abroad but would be gathered into one house. (They also knew that mankind should now understand the verse to indicate the gentiles *being not of this fold* to be included later as presented by Paul and not by the apostles. Any tribes still scattered would be of the Israelite fold. This was to be a major division in the truth.)

<sup>John 10:16 kjv 16</sup>And other sheep I have, *which are not of this fold*: them also I must bring, and they shall

hear my voice; and there shall be one-fold, and one shepherd.

The Committee mentioned that hidden in the clues was the two loaves of bread at the fulfillment of Pentecost and the two sticks becoming one in Ezekiel's prophesy concerning Israel. The ministry by Paul indicated one body for the mystery age of the church. A division of truth was indicated as discussed by the Committee and led into the mystery era to be discussed more later.

The Committee then looked at the ministry that had been fulfilled by the Communicator (Jesus as Christ) in the earthly mission. The ministry included much teaching, but the major focus of the sacrifice was the important item since the Israelites as a whole would reject Jesus. The Committee had recognized this rejection through their foreknowledge and had prepared their plan to take care of the rejection. Their plan including the cross had been foretold ahead of time with a few hidden details so that when the plan unfolded mankind should believe. One of the places the sacrifice of Jesus as the Lamb had been hidden was within a feast called the Passover. The Committee had presented the planned feast in the Word years before when the Israelite nation was coming out of Egypt. The procedure of this last plague had many representations in symbolism for mankind to easily understand once Jesus went to the cross. The Committee discussed the last plague using the sacrifice of a lamb and the use of the blood for the Israelites that believed. The blood was used as intended so the Israelites could escape death and be freed to go to the promised land. The Committee noted that mankind had understood the symbolism with songs written about the Lamb (Jesus) when He was crucified. They discussed and enjoyed the accomplishment of the redemption opportunity for mankind as planned.

**Jesus in some shadows:** Some of the shadows involved a hidden representation of Jesus and his life. As already mentioned, one of the shadows was the representation of Jesus as the Lamb for sacrifice. This representation came evident as Jesus became the true sacrifice and was then known as the true pure Lamb of sacrifice. The considered shadow was hidden as one of the plagues provided during the time of the exodus of the Israelites from Egypt as previously mentioned. The Committee was especially pleased with this shadow and its ease of understanding for mankind. A deeper understanding of this clue was the exodus revealing the salvation plan provided through the true crucifixion of Jesus on the Cross. The Israelites escaped the slavery position in Egypt by crossing the Red Sea to go to the promised Land. This shadow of the sacrificed lamb was to extend to mankind recognizing the true salvation plan as should be taught in the true churches and available in the Word for individual study. (Many of mankind had come to recognize the scenario of the Israelites physically coming out of Egypt on the way to the promised land and crossing the Jordan river as indicating the true journey from slavery of sin into heaven for those that believed Jesus was the real Lamb where the physical fulfilled the prophetic symbolism. The Committee agreed with this analogy. In particular the analogy of Elijah and Elisha was a deeper thought process for mankind to recognize.) This shadow of the lamb sacrifice and the extended meaning is currently still available and continuing to be protected in the recorded Word as follows:

> Exodus 12:1-36 kjv ¹And the LORD spake unto Moses and Aaron in the land of Egypt saying, ²This month shall be unto you the beginning of months: it shall be the first month of the year to you. ³Speak ye unto all the congregation of Israel, saying, In the tenth day of this month they shall take to them every man a lamb, according to the house of their fathers, a lamb for an house: ⁴And if the household be too little for the lamb, let him and his neighbour next unto his house take it according to the number of the souls; every man according to his eating shall make your count for the lamb. ⁵Your lamb shall be without blemish, a male of the first year: ye shall take it out from the sheep, or from the goats: ⁶And ye shall keep it up until the fourteenth day of the same month: and the whole assembly of the congregation of Israel shall kill it in the evening. ⁷And they shall take of the blood and strike it on the two side posts and on the upper door post of the houses, wherein they shall eat it. ⁸And they shall eat the flesh in that night, roast with fire, and unleavened bread; and with bitter herbs they shall eat it. ⁹Eat not of it raw, nor sodden at all with water, but roast with fire; his head with his legs, and with the purtenance thereof. ¹⁰And ye shall let nothing of it remain until the morning; and that which remaineth of it until the morning ye shall burn with fire. ¹¹And thus shall ye eat it; with your loins girded, your

shoes on your feet, and your staff in your hand; and ye shall eat it in haste: it is the LORD's passover. ¹²For I will pass through the land of Egypt this night, and will smite all the firstborn in the land of Egypt, both man and beast; and against all the gods of Egypt I will execute judgment: I am the LORD. ¹³And the blood shall be to you for a token upon the houses where ye are: and when I see the blood, I will pass over you, and the plague shall not be upon you to destroy you, when I smite the land of Egypt. ¹⁴And this day shall be unto you for a memorial; and ye shall keep it a feast to the LORD throughout your generations; ye shall keep it a feast by an ordinance forever. ¹⁵Seven days shall ye eat unleavened bread; even the first day ye shall put away leaven out of your houses: for whosoever eateth leavened bread from the first day until the seventh day, that soul shall be cut off from Israel. ¹⁶And in the first day there shall be an holy convocation, and in the seventh day there shall be an holy convocation to you; no manner of work shall be done in them, save that which every man must eat, that only may be done of you. ¹⁷And ye shall observe the feast of unleavened bread; for in this selfsame day have I brought your armies out of the land of Egypt: therefore, shall ye observe this day in your generations by an ordinance for ever. ¹⁸In the first month, on the fourteenth day of the month at even, ye shall eat unleavened bread, until the one and twentieth day of the month at even. ¹⁹Seven days shall there be no leaven found in your houses: for whosoever eateth that which is leavened, even that soul shall be cut off from the congregation of Israel, whether he be a stranger, or born in the land. ²⁰ Ye shall eat nothing leavened; in all your habitations shall ye eat unleavened bread. ²¹ Then Moses called for all the elders of Israel, and said unto them, Draw out and take you a lamb according to your families, and kill the passover. ²² And ye shall take a bunch of hyssop, and dip it in the blood that is in the bason, and strike the lintel and the two side posts with the blood that is in the bason; and none of you shall go out at the door of his house until the morning. ²³ For the LORD will pass through to smite the Egyptians; and when he seeth the blood upon the lintel, and on the two side posts, the LORD will pass over the door, and will not suffer the destroyer to come in unto your houses to smite you. ²⁴ And ye shall observe this thing for an ordinance to thee and to thy sons for ever. ²⁵ And it shall come to pass, when ye be come to the land which the LORD will give you, according as he hath promised, that ye shall keep this service. ²⁶ And it shall come to pass, when your children shall say unto you, What mean ye by this service? ²⁷ That ye shall say, It is the sacrifice of the LORD's passover, who passed over the houses of the children of Israel in Egypt, when he smote the Egyptians, and delivered our houses. And the people bowed the head and worshipped. ²⁸ And the children of Israel went away, and did as the LORD had commanded Moses and Aaron, so did they. ²⁹ And it came to pass, that at midnight the

LORD smote all the firstborn in the land of Egypt, from the firstborn of Pharaoh that sat on his throne unto the firstborn of the captive that was in the dungeon; and all the firstborn of cattle. ³⁰And Pharaoh rose up in the night, he, and all his servants, and all the Egyptians; and there was a great cry in Egypt; for there was not a house where there was not one dead. ³¹And he called for Moses and Aaron by night, and said, Rise up, and get you forth from among my people, both ye and the children of Israel; and go, serve the LORD, as ye have said. ³²Also take your flocks and your herds, as ye have said, and be gone; and bless me also. ³³And the Egyptians were urgent upon the people, that they might send them out of the land in haste; for they said, We be all dead men. ³⁴And the people took their dough before it was leavened, their kneading troughs being bound up in their clothes upon their shoulders. ³⁵And the children of Israel did according to the word of Moses; and they borrowed of the Egyptians jewels of silver, and jewels of gold, and raiment: ³⁶And the LORD gave the people favour in the sight of the Egyptians, so that they lent unto them such things as they required. And they spoiled the Egyptians.

The Committee continued to note the prophecy trail related to Jesus and his fulfillment of many prophecies. Another interesting fulfillment was the entry of Jesus on the donkey when entering Jerusalem during the week before His crucifixion. Again, the Committee had been careful to have this event told ahead of time and then fulfilled at a later time. The Committee knew that being able to provide these gaps of time between telling and fulfillment should be a truth that mankind would recognize and accept and believe as the Committee desired. An interesting concept about mankind and their free will that the Committee understood and had included in planning was the gap mankind seemed to have between the knowledge of knowing and still not believing. Mankind was and is missing the redemption truth by about 18 inches between their ability to know and their ability to believe. (This is the approximate distance between the mind to know and the heart to believe.) The Committee now looked at the fulfillment of the entry into Jerusalem following their plan to tell and then to fulfill so mankind would believe. The Committee could not believe that with the plan spelled out to mankind as in the Word and then fulfillment that yet mankind in general were continually ignoring the truth. The Committee discussed briefly a trait called ***mercy*** that they reserved for special occasions for mankind that truly did not have the opportunity to know and understand the Word.

*The Donkey Revealed:* This event is recorded in the Word as the prophecy of Zechariah and the fulfillment of the prophecy occurred over 400 years later.

> Zechariah 9:9 kjv 9 Rejoice greatly, O daughter of Zion; shout, O daughter of Jerusalem: behold, thy King cometh unto thee: he is just, and having salvation; lowly, and riding upon an ass, and upon a colt the foal of an ass.

<sup>Matthew 21:5 kjv 5</sup>Tell ye the daughter of Sion, Behold, thy King cometh unto thee, meek, and sitting upon an ass, and a colt the foal of an ass.

Jesus had continued to fulfill all the scriptures that the prophecies recorded referring to His earthly ministry. (The Committee discussed briefly about the prophecies He would fulfill after His earthly ministry in fulfilling the previously noted gap in Isaiah 61 among other events to come even now.) The Committee now turned their attention to some other fulfillments. The Psalms presentation of his death on the cross became a focus as one easy for mankind to understand.

**_Emphasizing the Important Body:_** As a result of the planned virgin birth and the unleavened body and blood, there was only one body prepared for the perfect sinless sacrifice. Jesus indicated this several ways in discussing the body. (One way was as the bread (unleavened) of life.) Already mentioned by the Committee, the plan had been recognized for mankind to understand early in the Word and revealed throughout due time. The Committee discussed the unleavened bread brought out of Egypt and with the children of Israel as they journeyed. Jesus had indicated that He was the bread of life. At the last supper Jesus had identified the bread as a symbol of his body to be broken. Thus, His body was a special fulfillment of the shadow symbol of unleavened bread. The real had been now shown to take the place of the symbol and this was one of the shadows that mankind was to understand and be responsible for accepting in belief. The Committee noted several truisms related to the specially prepared body. It was to accomplish a lasting sacrifice as the sacrifice of the animals were also shadows and temporary sacrifices before the true sacrifice came. Only the one special body and no other would satisfy as a substitute for all mankind's sin. The exchange was the righteousness of Jesus' perfect body along with His blood (pure of sin through the virgin birth) to take the place for all mankind's sin. The pure righteousness of Jesus through individual mankind's belief is to replace the true believer's attempt at righteousness when facing a future judgement.

> Isaiah 64:6 kjv 6But we are all as an unclean thing, and all our righteousnesses are as filthy rags; and we all do fade as a leaf; and our iniquites, like the wind, have taken us away.

Everyone could get free forgiveness of all sins if they believed as Abraham had. The same opportunity was and is now available for all that believe in the true sacrifice on the cross. The unleavened bread symbol and shadow now has been revealed with true substance in the specially prepared body of Jesus. (Again, the Committee noted the substance and evidence for true faith was continually being presented in the Word. In the final judgement, individual mankind with an opportunity to understand will have no excuse for unbelief. The foreknowledge and mercy of the Committee would be in place when needed.)

> Romans 9:15 kjv 15For he saith to Moses, I will have mercy on whom I will have mercy, and I will have compassion on whom I will have compassion.

The Committee discussed with the One with the now glorified body that He had explained this symbolic use of unleavened bread at the last supper indirectly to the apostles and to mankind. Even the apostles had failed to understand till a later time, but the shadow clue had been given with emphasis at the last supper.

> Matthew 26:26-28 kjv 26 And as they were eating, Jesus took bread, and blessed it, and brake it, and gave it to the disciples, and said, Take, eat; *this is my body*. 27 And he took the cup, and gave thanks, and gave it to them, saying, Drink ye all of it; 28 For *this is my blood of the new testament, which is shed for many for the remission of sins*.

> Hebrews 10:1-39 kjv 1 For the law having a shadow of good things to come, and not the very image of the things, can never with those sacrifices which they offered year by year continually make the comers thereunto perfect. 2 For then would they not have ceased to be offered? because that the worshippers once purged should have had no more conscience of sins. 3 But in those sacrifices, there is a remembrance again made of sins every year. 4 For it is not possible that the blood of bulls and of goats should take away sins. 5 *Wherefore when he cometh into the world, he saith, Sacrifice and offering thou wouldest not, but a body hast thou prepared me*: 6 In burnt offerings and sacrifices for sin thou hast had no pleasure. 7 Then said I, Lo, I come (in the volume of the book it is written of me,) to do thy will, O God. 8 Above when he said,

Sacrifice and offering and burnt offerings and offering for sin thou wouldest not, neither hadst pleasure therein; which are offered by the law; 9 Then said he, Lo, I come to do thy will, O God. He taketh away the first, that he may establish the second. 10 By the which will we are sanctified through the offering of the body of Jesus Christ once for all. 11 And every priest standeth daily ministering and offering oftentimes the same sacrifices, which can never take away sins: 12 But this man, after he had offered one sacrifice for sins forever, sat down on the right hand of God; 13 From henceforth expecting till his enemies be made his footstool. 14 For by one offering he hath perfected forever them that are sanctified. 15 Whereof the Holy Ghost also is a witness to us: for after that he had said before, 16 This is the covenant that I will make with them after those days, saith the Lord, I will put my laws into their hearts, and in their minds will I write them; 17 And their sins and iniquities will I remember no more. *18 Now where remission of these is, there is no more offering for sin.* 19 Having therefore, brethren, boldness to enter into the holiest by the blood of Jesus, 20 By a new and living way, which he hath consecrated for us, *through the veil, that is to say, his flesh;* 21 And having an high priest over the house of God; 22 Let us draw near with a true heart in full assurance of faith, having our hearts sprinkled from an evil conscience, and our bodies washed with pure water. 23 Let us hold fast the profession of our faith without wavering; (for he is faithful that promised;) ²⁴And let us consider one another to provoke unto love and to good works: ²⁵Not forsaking the assembling of ourselves together, as the manner of some is; but exhorting one another: and so much the more, as ye see the day approaching. ²⁶For if we sin willfully after that we have received the knowledge of the truth, there remaineth no more sacrifice for sins, ²⁷But a certain fearful looking for of judgment and fiery indignation, which shall devour the adversaries. ²⁸He that despised Moses' law died without mercy under two or three witnesses: ²⁹Of how much sorer punishment, suppose ye, shall he be thought worthy, who hath trodden underfoot the Son of God, and hath counted the blood of the covenant, wherewith he was sanctified, an unholy thing, and hath done despite unto the Spirit of grace? ³⁰For we know him that hath said, Vengeance belongeth unto me, I will recompense, saith the Lord. And again, The Lord shall judge his people. ³¹It is a fearful thing to fall into the hands of the living God. ³²But call to remembrance the former days, in which, after ye were illuminated, ye endured a great fight of afflictions; ³³Partly, whilst ye were made a gazingstock both by reproaches and afflictions; and partly, whilst ye became companions of them that were so used. ³⁴For ye had compassion of me in my bonds, and took joyfully the spoiling of your goods, knowing in yourselves that ye have in heaven a better and an enduring substance. ³⁵Cast not away therefore your confidence, which hath great recompence of reward. ³⁶For ye have need of patience, that, after ye have done the will of God, ye might receive the promise. ³⁷For yet a little while, and he that shall come will come, and will not tarry. ³⁸Now the just shall live by faith: but if any man draws back, my soul shall have no pleasure in him. ³⁹But we are not of them who draw back unto perdition; but of them that believe to the saving of the soul.

***The Death of Jesus:*** The Committee noted that the above recorded words provided evidence about the birth attributes of Jesus' life to support who He was. The recorded words also gave more evidence that was events told ahead so that when the events happened mankind should believe. These events detailed the death of Jesus. Thus, both the birth of Jesus as the Son and the death of Jesus along with His resurrection is established in history of the past at the current time. Psalms continues to unveil some definite details of the death on the cross through prophecy many years before the cross. After the cross mankind was and is to compare the prophecy with the fulfillment by Jesus in being sacrificed on the cross. Knowledge in the mind should lead into belief in the heart. The truth comes out of the shadows when mankind recognizes the fulfillment.

Psalms 22:1-31 kjv ¹My God, my God, why hast thou forsaken me? why art thou so far from helping me, and from the words of my roaring? ²O my God, I cry in the daytime, but thou hearest not; and in the night season, and am not silent. ³But thou art holy, O thou that inhabitest the praises of Israel. [4] Our fathers trusted in thee: they trusted, and thou didst deliver them. [5] They cried unto thee, and were delivered: they trusted in thee, and were not confounded. [6] But I am a worm, and no man; a reproach of men, and despised of the people. [7] All they that see me laugh me to scorn: they shoot out the lip, they shake the head, saying, [8] He trusted on the LORD that he would deliver him: let him deliver him, seeing he delighted in him. [9] But thou art he that took me out of the womb: thou didst make me hope when I was upon my mother's breasts. [10] I was cast upon thee from the womb: thou art my God from my mother's belly. [11] Be not far from me; for trouble is near; for there is none to help. [12] Many bulls have compassed me: strong bulls of Bashan have beset me round. [13] They gaped upon me with their mouths, as a ravening and a roaring lion. [14] I am poured out like water, and all my bones are out of joint: my heart is like wax; it is melted in the midst of my bowels. [15] My strength is dried up like a potsherd; and my tongue cleaveth to my jaws; and thou hast brought me into the dust of death. [16] For dogs have compassed me: the assembly of the wicked have inclosed me: they pierced my hands and my feet. [17] I may tell all my bones: they look and stare upon me. [18] They part my garments among them and cast lots upon my vesture. [19] But be not thou far from me, O LORD: O my strength, haste thee to help me. [20] Deliver my soul from the sword; my darling from the power of the dog. [21] Save me from the lion's mouth: for thou hast heard me from the horns of the unicorns. ²²I will declare thy name unto my brethren: in the midst of the congregation will I praise thee. ²³Ye that fear the LORD, praise him; all ye the seed of Jacob, glorify him; and fear him, all ye the seed of Israel. ²⁴For he hath not despised nor abhorred the affliction of the afflicted; neither hath he hid his face from him; but when he cried unto him, he heard. ²⁵My praise shall be of thee in the great congregation: I will pay my vows before them that fear him. ²⁶The meek shall eat and be satisfied: they shall praise the LORD that seek him: your heart shall live forever. ²⁷All the ends of the world shall remember and turn unto the LORD: and all the kindreds of the nations shall worship before thee. ²⁸For the kingdom is the LORD's: and he is the governor among the nations. ²⁹All they that be fat upon earth shall eat and worship: all they that go down to the dust shall bow before him: and none can keep alive his own soul. ³⁰A seed shall serve him; it shall be accounted to the Lord for a generation. ³¹They shall come and shall declare his righteousness unto a people that shall be born, that he hath done this.

The Committee then recalled how the prophet Isaiah presented Israel and the life of the Messiah in several chapters of the Word. They considered chapter 53 in relation to the fulfillment by Jesus. The Committee was interested in how their plan effected mankind's use of free will. The plan to present prophecy and then when it happened mankind was to begin to understand and form a substantive foundation to believe. They noted that often the prophets and even the disciples did not understand the prophecy except when fulfillment happened in their time, Currently, mankind had a deeper meaning available to them as time revealed more fulfillment of prophecy. After the cross, a new and greater meaning was available to mankind than before the cross.

Isaiah 53:1-12 kjv 1 Who hath believed our report? and to whom is the arm of the LORD revealed? 2 For he shall grow up before him as a tender plant, and as a root out of a dry ground: he hath no form nor comeliness; and when we shall see him, there is no beauty that we should desire him. 3 He is despised and rejected of men; a man of sorrows, and acquainted with grief: and we hid as it were our faces from him; he was despised, and we esteemed him not. 4 Surely he hath borne our griefs, and carried our sorrows: yet we did esteem him stricken, smitten of God, and afflicted. 5 But he was wounded for our transgressions, he was bruised for our iniquities: the chastisement of our peace was upon him; and with his stripes we are healed. 6 All we like sheep have gone astray; we have turned everyone to his own way; and the LORD hath laid on him the iniquity of us all. 7 He was oppressed, and he was afflicted, yet he opened not his mouth: he is brought as a lamb to the slaughter, and as a sheep before her shearers is dumb, so he openeth not his mouth. 8 He was taken from prison and from judgment: and who shall declare his generation? for he was cut off out of the land of the living: for the transgression of my people was he stricken. ⁹And he made his grave with the wicked, and with the rich in his death; because he had done no violence, neither was any deceit in his mouth. ¹⁰Yet it pleased the LORD to bruise him; he hath put him to grief: when thou shalt make his soul an offering for sin, he shall see his seed, he shall prolong his days, and the pleasure of the LORD shall prosper in his hand. ¹¹He shall see of the travail of his soul, and shall be satisfied: by his knowledge shall my righteous servant justify many; for he shall bear their iniquities. ¹²Therefore will I divide him a portion with the great, and he shall divide the spoil with the strong; because he hath poured out his soul unto death: and he was numbered with the transgressors; and he bare the sin of many, and made intercession for the transgressors.

The Committee discussed the fulfillment of Jesus in the prophecy. He was numbered between two thieves. It was noted that some of the Word was linked as in the prophecy where He was cut off and here, He was also cut off. Both times not for His self. Note that Daniel had a difficult time understanding in His time all the prophecy. Likewise: Some of the prophetic Word related to week seventy is still left for mankind to consider. However, the Committee continued to discuss that everything prophesied in the Word had come true as time revealed so faith centered on the belief that the Word would continue to be fulfilled in its completion.

*The Plan Being Successful:* The Committee considered that even the apostles that were with Jesus did not understand some of what He taught them. This was also recorded in the Word so mankind could understand the plan and take advantage of this understanding of the Committee's plan. An example is found in the Word as follows. It was noted several times so the disciples would remember that there were communications of Jesus that they did not understand. As the Committee had planned, the disciples believed when that saw what Jesus taught unfold in their future. The following discussion resulted among Jesus and his disciples.

> Matthew 15:15-16 kjv 15 Then answered Peter and said unto him, Declare unto us this parable. 16 And Jesus said, Are ye also yet without understanding?

The Committee noted that often Jesus had to explain the meaning behind the symbolism and the hidden meaning for even the disciples to understand. Several examples of Jesus explaining the revealing of meaning was presented for the disciples (and for mankind) in the scriptures. One of these related to symbolism of the two events in loaves of bread as recorded in Mathew 16.

> Matthew 16:9-12 kjv 9 Do ye not yet **understand**, neither remember the five loaves of the five thousand, and how many baskets ye took up? 10 Neither the seven loaves of the four thousand, and how many baskets ye took up? 11 How is it that ye do not understand that I spake it not to you concerning bread, that ye should beware of the leaven of the Pharisees and

of the Sadducees? ¹²Then understood they how that he bade them not beware of the leaven of bread, but of the doctrine of the Pharisees and of the Sadducees.

As the Committee came to discuss the life of Jesus, they began to recall many shadows of Jesus as revealed in the Word by prophesy or even directly by Jesus beyond that already discussed in their current meeting. The most important events were those related to the virgin birth along with the sacrificial death on the cross followed by the burial and resurrection. The birth and death as to place, parents, and lineage as foretold of Jesus was and is to be considered by mankind. Foretelling these two events (the virgin birth and the sacrificial death on the cross) prior to one's life is impossible for mankind. The ability to tell of the birth and death of Jesus ahead of the events certainly should indicate the Committee having foreknowledge to use in making their plan. (Remembering the plan was, is, and continues to provide mankind with information so when it does come to pass, mankind should believe in the redemption plan provided through the death, burial, and resurrection of Jesus. The disciples provided evidence that the plan was working as when they saw fulfillment . . . they believed . . . the committee noted that substance of the physical events was a powerful foundation for belief. The Word also recorded this substantial foundation in Hebrews 11 as the Word defined faith in moving from the physical seen into belief of the unseen. This change in belief continued to be the goal of the plan.) The Committee's plan continues to add substance and evidence as time passed.

Hebrews 11:1 kjv 1 Now *faith is the substance* of things hoped for, the *evidence of things not seen.*

The Committee was pleased with this evidence as indicated at the empty tomb and later faith and belief shown by the actions of the apostles. The Word recorded that Jesus had revealed His future time in the tomb and that the disciples did not believe until they saw the real event.

The Committee discussed the napkin about Jesus' face when buried as in the case of Lazarus in the Word and then the removal and folding as indicated in the tomb of Jesus. These two events were in the Word also for mankind to consider as did John. Seeing the real event provided more substance and more evidence to John in creating a greater faith and believing of the unseen.

The Committee considered the following sequence teaching by Jesus:

> Luke 9:20-22 kjv 20 He said unto them, but whom say ye that I am? Peter answering said, The Christ of God. 21 And he straitly charged them, and commanded them to tell no man that thing; 22 Saying, The Son of man must suffer many things, and *be rejected of the elders and chief priests and scribes, and be slain, and be raised the third day.*

For Lazarus:

> John 11:44 kjv 44 And he that was dead came forth, bound hand and foot with graveclothes: and his face was

bound about with a **napkin**. Jesus saith unto them, loose him, and let him go.

For Jesus:

> John 20:7-9 kjv 7 And the napkin, that was about his head, not lying with the linen clothes, but wrapped together in a place by itself. 8 ***Then went in also that other disciple, which came first to the sepulchre, and he saw, and believed.*** *9 For as yet they knew not the scripture, that he must rise again from the dead.*

Hence, the disciples gained belief based on seeing the physical fulfillment of what Jesus had been teaching them as they traveled with Him. This prepared the disciples for the receiving of the Comforter (Holy Spirit) in fulfillment of the Feast of Pentecost as taught by Jesus. Among the shadows for mankind to observe and understand were shadows that should be easy to understand once seen. The Committee expressed hopes that as John had seen the folded napkin in the empty tomb and what Jesus had taught became real to him . . . so it should be to most mankind. The Committee continued to discuss that although the apostles had traveled with Jesus and heard His teachings, Jesus and the Committee realized that telling was not understood by the apostles until the apostles saw it physically happen. The Committee noted that mankind is doing the same thing today. They may be reading but without seeing the physical experience mankind continues to have a hard time recognizing the truth. Faith is needed. Faith is belief without seeing the physical event to be believed. (The Committee noted that many physical events from prophesy had happened recently (in relation to Israel becoming a nation and Jerusalem being recognized as the capital in particular) but mankind was seemingly blinded to belief. Many of mankind seemed to lack the knowledge of the Word in order to link the experience with the Word. Thus, mankind was ignorant of the events being foretold and only a few enjoyed and understood the experiences of fulfillment of prophecy or the teachings of Jesus. The Committee noted that the early Christians had zeal but lacked knowledge. Now the opportunity for Word knowledge was increased as indicated in the Word of prophesy in Daniel but mankind seemed to lack the attention and therefore the zeal.)

The experience needed for the plan to work was not noted by most of mankind. The Committee noted that sad as it might be, their foreknowledge had viewed these phenomena. The Committee also noted that their total plan as recorded in the Word would be completed as written.

**_Shadows of the Resurrection:_** The Committee now turned to other shadows of Jesus and his resurrection. The Committee discussed limiting the events related to the resurrection as they had previously done in discussing the physical life of Jesus. The Word reminded all that books could not hold all that Jesus had done. Hence, only a few fulfillments were to be discussed in this meeting.

> John 21:25 kjv 25 And there are also many other things which Jesus did, the which, if they should be written

everyone, I suppose that even the world itself could not contain the **books** that should be written. Amen

*The Shadow of Jonah:* The Committee considered the words of Jesus in explaining the sign of Jonah. They noted the plan of explaining the meaning ahead of time so that when the plan was completed all mankind would have an opportunity to understand and believe. Note that Jesus was explaining the meaning before the three days in the tomb as presently known. Thus, mankind at this present time has continued to have a greater opportunity to understand and believe. The event had been explained and was fulfilled in the past as planned for mankind to see, understand, and believe. Note the stern admonition by Jesus about the expectation for mankind to understand and respond.

> Matthew 12:38-42 kjv 38 Then certain of the scribes and of the Pharisees answered, saying, Master, we would see a sign from thee. 39 But he answered and said unto them, An evil and adulterous generation seeketh after a sign; and there shall no sign be given to it, but the sign of the prophet Jonas: 40 For as Jonas was three days and three nights in the whale's belly; so shall the Son of man be three days and three nights in the heart of the earth. *41 The men of Nineveh shall rise in judgment with this generation, and shall condemn it: because they repented at the preaching of Jonas; and, behold, a greater than Jonas is here. 42 The queen of the south shall rise up in the judgment with this*

> *generation, and shall condemn it: for she came from the uttermost parts of the earth to hear the wisdom of Solomon; and, behold, a greater than Solomon is here.*

The Committee noted that most of mankind seemed to understand the connection of the three days of Jonah as a sign of Jesus being three days in the tomb. However, the sign did not stop there as it extended into the result of being in the belly of the fish. After the three days in the fish, Jonah continued to present a message to the gentiles of Nineveh. This message resulted in the people repenting. Thus, after the three days in the tomb, the sign was not to stop but extend into a message to be unveiled to ***gentiles***. This was a mystery to be declared by Paul as Jonah had tried to reject it. (The Committee discussed the shadow of Jonah as an Israelite after three days in the belly of the whale took the message to the gentiles. Jesus as an Israelite after three days in the belly of the earth provided the redemptive plan to the gentiles through Paul.

In particular, Jesus fulfilled three of the feasts set up by the Committee. Jesus fulfilled the Feast of Passover, the Feast of Unleavened Bread, and the Feast of First Fruits in His death, burial, and resurrection.

*First fruits: Facing Death-The First Time:* The feast of first fruits has been fulfilled!!! The harvest of fruits from the fig tree continued to have a hidden meaning representing a fulfillment through the nation of Israel. Jesus was a descendant of the tribe of Juda and represented a fruit from the true vine as He indicated in

His teaching. He did something that as a member of the Committee was special in becoming the true first fruit.

(Note: This was the first time a member of the Committee had taken on a mankind body and faced death with the intention to be raised and having His body changed into a glorified body. This would be the first glorified body changed (not replaced). In nature was several changes of form as in the butterfly cycle for mankind to experience and gain knowledge related to this phenomenon.)

***A Special Death***: The Committee noted the facts behind the true death of the perfect body as sacrifice. The Committee noted that Jesus had no Adamic sin contamination due to the virgin birth. Therefore, His prepared body as indicated in Hebrews was a pure sacrifice in blood and body. ***Hence the wages of sin to bring on the first or second death was not in play***. Hence, Jesus was faced with the decision of His own free will to give up the ghost to die. (This action of free will was one that the Committee desired for mankind to understand along with its importance.) He chose to do so. In this action, He chose to be the perfect sacrifice and earn the right to substitute His perfect righteousness out of love for each individual descendant of Adam. The substitution of His death and righteousness without sin amounted to forgiveness of each mankind's sin since the cross including Adam and Eve. This substitution occurred if an individual mankind believed in His work on the cross. Most mankind seems to not have recognized the responsibility of Jesus in setting this example in use of His free will to choose to go to the cross. (The Committee also noted that some individual mankind had believed in the Committee through faith before the cross. Abraham had been an example with others mentioned in the Word.

> Luke 23:44-47 kjv 44 And it was about the sixth hour, and there was a darkness over all the earth until the ninth hour. 45 And the sun was darkened, and the veil of the temple was rent in the midst. 46 And when Jesus had cried with a loud voice, he said, Father, into thy hands I commend my spirit: and having said thus, he gave up the ghost. 47 Now when the centurion saw what was done, he glorified God, saying, certainly this was a righteous man.

**_Revelation in Nature:_** The Committee noted that mankind was given several natural physical representations of the changing of form. (Several shadows of representations in natural changes reflected a changing form in the life cycle.) Most prominent were biological changes studied by mankind. Among the most common was the changing of the body of a locust, of a frog, or of a butterfly. Noteworthy about the original body of these creatures was that their original physical body **_was not replaced but was changed_**. The outcome in each case was a body with different characteristics than the original body. Mankind should see and recognize the changing cycles of the butterfly going from a worm like body into a closure (tomb) and coming out as a beautiful form. So was the body of Jesus _not replaced but it was changed from an earthly body to one that became the glorified body_. The glorified body was not the spiritual form originally that Jesus had in the beginning at creation. Most mankind seems to think that in the death, burial, and resurrection the body is replaced when in reality it is changed. Note that Adam's physical body was not replaced but mysteriously changed due to the wages of sin and therefore faced the two deaths. (The physical death of the body and the eternal death recognized as a separation from eternal life with the Committee represent the two deaths.) For Jesus, His newly formed body kept some characteristics of His original earthly body but also took on some new characteristics to create His glorified body. As a member of the Committee He currently still has the glorified body and was recognizable by mankind as He visited mankind for forty days after His resurrection. Foreknowledge had been involved in the creation of original mankind in the image of the Communicator as planned by the Committee in looking forward to the change at the cross. The Committee noted the fulfillment of their plan through the changes and accomplishments by the Communicator at the cross and beyond.

The Committee discussed another event that happened as a result of the cross and the three days in the tomb. This event fulfilled scripture and supported the shadowing of an important change during the transition period of the cross. The veil in the tabernacle (temple) was rent in the middle from top to the bottom. This veil was the division in the tabernacle between the holy and the most holy place. Once it was torn down then this division between where the Committee dwelt, and mankind was removed based on the new covenant. The Word in Hebrews explained this veil of division as being flesh. Jesus removed this division of flesh and created an opening. He immediately became the first fruit at His resurrection. Then some of the saints that slept came forth while paradise was moved to a heavenly location.

> **The First fruits:** <sub>Matthew 27:50-53 kjv 50</sub>Jesus, when he had cried again with a loud voice, yielded up the ghost. <sup>51</sup> And, behold, the veil of the temple was rent in twain from the top to the bottom; and the earth did quake, and the rocks rent; <sup>52</sup>And the graves were opened; and many bodies of the saints which slept arose, <sup>53</sup>And came out of the graves *after his resurrection*, and went into the holy city, and appeared unto many.
> <sub>Hebrews 10:19-22 kjv 19</sub>Having therefore, brethren, boldness to enter into the holiest by *the blood* of Jesus, <sup>20</sup>By a new and living way, which he hath consecrated for us, through the veil, that is to say*, his flesh*; <sup>21</sup>And having an high priest over the house of God; <sup>22</sup>Let us draw near with a true heart in full assurance of faith, having our hearts sprinkled from an evil conscience, and our bodies washed with pure water.
>
> <sub>Romans 8:29 kjv 29</sub>For whom he did foreknow, he also did predestinate to be conformed to the image of his Son, that he might be the firstborn among many brethren.

The Committee discussed an important detail that mankind might should recognize. The graves being opened and many of the saints rising did not involve the saints being joined with the redemption of their bodies. The saints now became firstfruits of the Spirit as indicated in a later teaching of Paul. When mankind dies they become a fruit of the Spirit and will later enjoy a redemption of individual bodies as celestial bodies. Jesus as the first fruit and needing to testify of the celestial body for forty days received His.

> Romans 8:23 kjv 23And not only they, but ourselves also, which have the firstfruits of the Spirit, even we ourselves groan within ourselves, waiting for the adoption, to wit, the redemption of our **body**.

Removing the veil removed the separation of the most holy from the holy. This let the most holy associate with mankind for the first time since in the Garden of Eden. (The Comforter (Holy Spirit as a member of the Committee of three) has been sent by the Father (a member of the Committee of three) as Jesus (a member of the Committee of three) had indicated during his earthly ministry. The Comforter now moves within believing mankind to indwell within the tabernacle (body) of individual mankind based on individual mankind's belief.) The Committee noted that the joining of the Comforter to pass through the flesh had now happened since the work of Jesus on the cross. Belief in Jesus as the current true savior provides the Comforter (Holy Spirit) the opportunity to enter through the flesh of the believer. This reunion was also a mystery not yet explained. However, faith and belief still remain as the key to the Comforter (Holy Spirit) passing through the true veil (flesh).

*Out of the Shadows*

2 Corinthians 3:13-16 kjv 13And not as Moses, which put a veil over his face, that the children of Israel could not stedfastly look to the end of that which is abolished: 14But their minds were blinded: for until this day remaineth the same vail untaken away in the reading of the old testament; which vail is done away in Christ. 15But even unto this day, when Moses is read, the vail is upon their heart. 16Nevertheless when it shall turn to the Lord, the vail shall be taken away.

John 14:16 kjv 16And I will pray the Father, and he shall give you another **Comforter**, that he may abide with you for ever;
John 14:26 kjv 26But the **Comforter**, which is the **Holy Ghost**, whom the Father will send in my name, he shall teach you all things, and bring all things to your remembrance, whatsoever I have said unto you.
John 15:26 kjv26But when the **Comforter** is come, whom I will send unto you from the Father, even the Spirit of truth, which proceedeth from the Father, he shall testify of me:
John 16:7 kjv 7Nevertheless I tell you the truth; It is expedient for you that I go away: for if I go not away, the **Comforter** will not come unto you; but if I depart, I will send him unto you.

**<u>The Committee noted the changing of the circumcision instituted to the Israelites in the first covenant to the inward circumcision of the heart. This change had been</u>**

***first presented in Jeremiah 31:31-32 in the Word and discussed previously.***

> Romans 2:28-29 kjv ²⁸For he is not a Jew, which is one outwardly; neither is that **circumcision**, which is outward in the flesh: ²⁹But he is a Jew, which is one inwardly; and circumcision is that of the heart, in the **spirit**, and not in the letter; whose praise is not of men, but of God.

The Committee discussed faith and belief as the center for acceptance of mankind. Faith and belief provided righteousness for Abraham before the law and before the cross and with individual mankind after the cross. Faith in the work of Jesus on the cross continues to provide a substitute for sin. The burial and resurrection of Jesus is the hope for mankind. Many of mankind have not accepted that some Jews are of faith even though continuing under the law as before the cross with circumcision of the first covenant and many Jews and gentiles are of faith under circumcision of the heart after Jesus. This is a division of the truth illustrated by the ministry of the twelve disciples to the Israelites under the first covenant and the ministry of Paul under the new covenant. Both covenants remain in effect as planned by the Committee. Both are based on individual belief according to the directions for the twelve and according to the direction for Paul. (Both covenants remain in effect today even though mankind may not accept this plan. This continuation of both covenants supports the plan for the division of time noted between the rapture and the seventieth week of Daniel and the completion of the blindness of Israel during the seventieth week.) Again, belief is the key for the Committee. Faith was possible under each covenant. As mankind may consider . . . Those under the first covenant of circumcision (As with Abraham had faith) would be "grandfathered" in. In the Word, the Committee made a clue of truth and difference in the statements "circumcision **by** faith" of the first covenant and "uncircumcision **through** faith" of the second covenant. (In general, circumcision means Israelite and uncircumcision indicates gentiles.)

> Romans 3:30 kjv 30 Seeing it is one God, which shall justify the **circumcision** <u>by faith</u>, and **uncircumcision** <u>through faith</u>.

> Galatians 5:6 kjv 6 For in Jesus Christ neither **circumcision** availeth anything, nor uncircumcision; but faith which worketh by love.

The Committee noted that in the tabernacle design was an important mercy seat within the veil set up by directions given to Moses. Although mankind had not paid much attention to the <u>*mercy*</u> characteristic of the Committee, the Committee recognized this attribute and has continued to use it throughout history.

> Romans 9:15-16 kjv 15 For he saith to Moses, I will have **mercy** on whom I will have **mercy**, and I will have compassion on whom I will have compassion. So, then it is not of him that willeth, nor of him that runneth, but of God that sheweth **mercy**.

> Romans 9:18 kjv 18 Therefore hath he **mercy** on whom he will have **mercy**, and whom he will he hardeneth.

***Appearances***: The Committee observed that in His glorified body Jesus was recognized and joined mankind and the apostles in several appearances between his coming out of the tomb and his final ascension to take his seat in the heavens. Two major experiences to increase knowledge and belief was He had overcome death and, in His resurrection, had changed his body into the glorified body that still maintained many of the physical functions as was a part of the original human body. This provided more evidence that mankind was originally made in the image of the Committee and in the image of the glorified body. The original body of Adam and Eve (and following descendants) were changed due to the future physical death they experienced when disobeying in the Garden of Eden. Through sin Adam and Eve lost eternal physical life through a sin change in many of the original created body characteristics. Now Jesus as the first fruits had restored hope by mankind who believed to gain the glorified body. The Committee noted that many of mankind had continued to seek after becoming as an angel, but this is a major reason for correctly dividing the truth. Angels are of a different creation than mankind. Mankind does not become an angel in physical death.

*The Comforter*: Jesus in his teaching ministry had indicated the coming of a Comforter after He had left. As indicated above, the apostles listened and heard but did not understand as Jesus was telling about events to happen in the future. The Comforter was not understood at the time as Jesus taught. The disciples had not understood about the death, burial, and the resurrection. Jesus ascended into the heavens and then at the coming Feast of Pentecost, the Comforter identified as the Holy Ghost ascended to be a down payment unto the day of redemption.

> John 7:39 kjv 39(But this spake he of the **Spirit**, which they that believe on him should receive: for the **Holy Ghost** was not yet given; because that Jesus was not yet glorified.)

> Ephesians 1:13 kjv 13In whom ye also trusted, after that ye heard the word of truth, the gospel of your salvation: in whom also after that ye believed, ye were sealed with that **holy Spirit** of promise,

> Ephesians 4:30 kjv 30And grieve not the **holy Spirit** of God, whereby ye are sealed unto the day of redemption.

> 2 Corinthians 1:21-22 kjv 21Now he which stablisheth us with you in Christ, and hath anointed us, is God; 22 Who hath also sealed us, and given the earnest of the Spirit in our hearts.

**_Fulfillment of Feasts:_** Two of the major feasts involved the Passover (Representing the sacrifice of the Lamb and fulfilled with the sacrifice of Jesus on the cross) and the Pentecost (Representing fulfillment with the Comforter descending as Jesus had foretold). Hidden was the Feast of Tabernacles being at the time of the virgin birth of Jesus. This feast was fulfilled to some extent where the baby Jesus was the beginning of the tabernacle being represented as the temple. Note that this fit the comments of Jesus about the temple as a tabernacle and His body being a representation of a Tabernacle. Hence the

Tabernacle was a special shadow representation, and this indicated why the Committee had taken such care in its construction when directing the structure to Moses. The finishing of fulfillment of this feast is to be at a future time.

> John 2:19-20 kjv ¹⁹Jesus answered and said unto them, Destroy this temple, and in **three days** I will raise it up. ²⁰Then said the Jews, Forty and six years was this temple in building, and wilt thou rear it up in **three days**?

> I Corinthians 3:16 kjv ¹⁶Know ye not that ye are the temple of God, and that the **Spirit** of God dwelleth in you?

Again, the Committee noted that the Jews at their time did not understand but the plan for understanding was in the future. As John and the other apostles along with mankind onward and even to the present and future time understanding should be evidenced. Simply the tabernacle (temple) was represented by the body of Jesus. His tabernacle (body) was rebuilt in three days to become His glorified body,

***The Hidden Shadow of the Seed:*** The seed of woman as indicated in Genesis (stated and considered by the Committee) created the generation of Jesus. The Committee noted this as being indicated in the genealogies in Mathew and Luke. Thus, one needs to consider the generation of Jesus. Consider the changed resurrection and glorified body as a result of this seed developed generation. Consider the new births indicated in the Word to Nicodemus (John chapter 3) as being in the generation of Jesus. Mankind are often found discussing *the last generation based on the scriptures*. ***The generation of Jesus through being born again as introduced to Nicodemus --will never end so it is the last generation***. The Committee discussed that mankind should simply chase the seed throughout the Word to better understand the seed and the lasting generation of Jesus.

<sub>Revelation 12:1-17 kjv</sub> ¹And there appeared a great wonder in heaven; a woman clothed with the sun, and the moon under her feet, and upon her head a crown of twelve stars: ²And she being with child cried, travailing in birth, and pained to be delivered. ³And there appeared another wonder in heaven; and behold a great red dragon, having seven heads and ten horns, and seven crowns upon his heads. ⁴And his tail drew the third part of the stars of heaven, and did cast them to the earth: and the dragon stood before the woman, which was ready to be delivered, for to devour her child as soon as it was born. ⁵And she brought forth a man child, who was to rule all nations with a rod of iron: and her child was caught up unto God, and to his throne. ⁶And the woman fled into the wilderness, where she hath a place prepared of God, that they should feed her there a thousand two hundred and threescore days. ⁷And there was war in heaven: Michael and his angels fought against the dragon; and the dragon fought and his angels, ⁸And prevailed not; neither was their place found any more in heaven. ⁹And the great dragon was cast out, that old serpent, called the Devil, and

Satan, which deceiveth the whole world: he was cast out into the earth, and his angels were cast out with him. ¹⁰And I heard a loud voice saying in heaven, Now is come salvation, and strength, and the kingdom of our God, and the power of his Christ: for the accuser of our brethren is cast down, which accused them before our God day and night. ¹¹And they overcame him by the blood of the Lamb, and by the word of their testimony; and they loved not their lives unto the death. ¹²Therefore rejoice, ye heavens, and ye that dwell in them. Woe to the inhabiters of the earth and of the sea! for the devil is come down unto you, having great wrath, because he knoweth that he hath but a short time. ¹³And when the dragon saw that he was cast unto the earth, he persecuted the woman which brought forth the man child. ¹⁴And to the woman were given two wings of a great eagle, that she might fly into the wilderness, into her place, where she is nourished for a time, and times, and half a time, from the face of the serpent. ¹⁵And the serpent cast out of his mouth water as a flood after the woman, that he might cause her to be carried away of the flood. ¹⁶And the earth helped the woman, and the earth opened her mouth, and swallowed up the flood which the dragon cast out of his mouth. ¹⁷And the dragon was wroth with the woman, and went to make war with the remnant of ***her seed,*** which keep the commandments of God, and have the testimony of Jesus Christ.

(The Committee noted that there were several time gaps in this chapter of the Word but they decided mankind could understand easily the overall prophetic meaning. Joseph's dreams should help.)

The Committee recognized that mankind now had this revelation that Israel represented the mother in their plan and Jesus was to be their representative. A dream of Joseph now extended the symbols to still represent the nation of Israel. The virgin birth had now happened, and the Adamic sin had not been transferred so that Jesus would not have the contaminated blood line since the Adamic sin was determined by the decision made by Adam of his own free will. The plan was now in place and mankind had the opportunity in accepting the offer of a new birth described in the Word and recorded in John 1-3 to Nicodemus. This new birth was also a mystery to be learned through study. The Committee jumped back to a mystery being revealed at the current time and presented by Isaiah. How could the birth pains be after the birth? The Committee was amused at mankind figuring out this mystery and some not recognizing it as inspirational motivation by one of their members of mankind being guided by the Committee.

**The Committee recognized A deeper meaning was still hidden by the travail of birth and to be unveiled soon.**

*<u>New Covenant:</u>* Between the Communicator and all mankind, the cross and the meaning of Jesus' death, burial, and resurrection in fulfilment of Jeremiah's prophetical shadow in the Old Testament Word has now been revealed. The Committee noted that this new

covenant was for the total nation of Israel which included the ten tribes of the Southern Kingdom (Israel) united with the two tribes of the Northern Kingdom (Judea). (This united nation of Israel has been established in these end times being discussed and is a major sign for mankind to understand.)

> <sup>Jeremiah 31:31-34 kjv 31</sup>Behold, the days come, saith the LORD, that I will make a new covenant with the house of Israel, and with the house of Judah: <sup>32</sup>Not according to the <u>covenant that I made with their fathers in the day that I took them by the hand to bring them out of the land of Egypt</u>; which my covenant they brake, although I was *an husband* unto them, saith the LORD: <sup>33</sup>But this shall be the covenant that I will make with the house of Israel; After those days, saith the LORD, I will put my law <u>in their inward parts</u>, and write it in their hearts; and will be their God, and they shall be my people. <sup>34</sup>And they shall teach no more every man his neighbour, and every man his brother, saying, Know the LORD: for they shall all know me, from the least of them unto the greatest of them, saith the LORD: for I will forgive their iniquity, and I will remember their sin no more.

(The Committee briefly commented on two hidden shadows used in this prophecy that had now been revealed and discussed. Being the husband of the nation of Israel revealed the virgin birth of Jesus by the wife and mother symbol of Israel as indicated in chapter 12 of Revelations in the Word. (See chapter 12 previously given in this report.) Also, another hidden shadow in the Word was the indication of the indwelling of the Holy Spirit fulfilled since Pentecost.)

The Committee noted that the bridge between these two covenants was presented in the Word through various methods. One of these methods was through the sequence of explanation in the Word as found in Hebrews chapters 9 and 10. The Committee continued to discuss how the shadows were beginning to converge as a major truth and fit together to represent the unconditional truth of their planned destiny for mankind based on the original plan of faith.

> Hebrews 9:1-28 kjv ¹Then verily the first covenant had also ordinances of divine service, and a worldly sanctuary. ²For there was a tabernacle made; the first, wherein was the candlestick, and the table, and the shewbread; which is called the sanctuary. ³And after the second veil, the tabernacle which is called the Holiest of all; ⁴Which had the golden censer, and the ark of the covenant overlaid round about with gold, wherein was the golden pot that had manna, and Aaron's rod that budded, and the tables of the covenant; ⁵And over it the cherubims of glory shadowing the mercyseat; of which we cannot now speak particularly. ⁶Now when these things were thus ordained, the priests went always into the first tabernacle, accomplishing the service of God. ⁷But into the second went the high priest alone once every year, not without blood, which he offered for himself, and for the errors of the people: ⁸*The Holy Ghost this signifying, that the*

*way into the holiest of all was not yet made manifest, while as the first tabernacle was yet standing*: ⁹Which was a figure for the time then present, in which were offered both gifts and sacrifices, that could not make him that did the service perfect, as pertaining to the conscience; ¹⁰Which stood only in meats and drinks, and divers washings, and carnal ordinances, imposed on them until the time of reformation. ¹¹But Christ being come an high priest of good things to come, by a greater and more perfect tabernacle, not made with hands, that is to say, not of this building; ¹²Neither by the blood of goats and calves, but by his own blood he entered in once into the holy place, having obtained eternal redemption for us. ¹³For if the blood of bulls and of goats, and the ashes of an heifer sprinkling the unclean, sanctifieth to the purifying of the flesh: ¹⁴How much more shall the blood of Christ, who through the eternal Spirit offered himself without spot to God, purge your conscience from dead works to serve the living God? ¹⁵And for this cause he is the mediator of the new testament, that by means of death, for the redemption of the transgressions that were under the first testament, they which are called might receive the promise of eternal inheritance. ¹⁶*For where a testament is, there must also of necessity be the death of the testator.* ¹⁷*For a testament is of force after men are dead: otherwise it is of no strength at all while the testator liveth*. ¹⁸Whereupon neither the first testament was dedicated without blood. ¹⁹For when Moses had spoken every precept to all the people according to the law, he took the blood of calves and of goats, with water, and scarlet wool, and hyssop, and sprinkled both the book, and all the people, ²⁰Saying, This is the blood of the testament which God hath enjoined unto you. ²¹Moreover he sprinkled with blood both the tabernacle, and all the vessels of the ministry. ²²And almost all things are by the law purged with blood; and <u>without shedding of blood is no remission.</u> ²³It was therefore necessary that the <u>patterns of things in the heavens should be purified with these; but the heavenly things themselves with better sacrifices than these. ²⁴For Christ is not entered into the holy places made with hands, which are the figures of the true; but into heaven itself, now to appear in the presence of God for us:</u> ²⁵Nor yet that he should offer himself often, as the high priest entereth into the holy place every year with blood of others; ²⁶For then must he often have suffered since the foundation of the world: but now **_once_** in the end of the world hath he appeared to put away sin by the sacrifice of himself. ²⁷And as it is appointed unto men once to die, but after this the judgment: ²⁸So Christ was **_once offered to bear the sins of many_**; and unto them that look for him shall he appear the second time without sin unto salvation.

(Hidden in this passage of the Word the Committee noted two major truths. No other sacrifice would be given as the true sacrifice had now been given and only once. Another hidden truth that became evidence was that sin through Satan had also contaminated the heavenly creation as well as that of the world. Hence, the plan of the free will offering of Jesus to become not only the pure sacrifice on the cross but also the true priest and eventually in the future to be a king of the world kingdom of nations including the purification of both the earth and the heavens. Remember in the Word the first verse stated by the Committee was "In the beginning God created the heavens and the earth." Thus, the Committee had a hidden clue even in the first verse of the Word.)

The Committee noted that Abraham's righteousness was not his own but established by his acceptance of and belief in the Communicator (Jesus the Messiah). This righteousness was not established by the law or performance of mankind because of work but established by the substitution on the cross. Jesus had substituted His pure righteousness for the forgiveness of sins of ALL mankind past, present, and future. Acceptance of this performance by Jesus of His own free will giving up the ghost now included the performance of mankind based on belief. This division between acceptable work of love based on belief and unacceptable work by mankind in order to earn the right to go to heaven in the eyes of the Committee was an important division. The work to earn mankind the right to only believe and enter heaven was finished as Jesus had indicated on the cross. Mankind was to discern the difference based on the position individually determined by appropriate acceptable belief. Daniel's decision and position in Daniel 1:8 kjv was cited as an excellent example. The Committee recognized that purpose and determination had been indicated by Daniel and these two traits continue to be great factors in believers.

> Daniel 1:8 kjv 8 But Daniel purposed in his heart that he would not defile himself with the portion of the king's meat, nor with the wine which he drank: therefore, he requested of the prince of the eunuchs that he might not defile himself.

Hebrews chapter 11 in the recorded Word was intended to provide mankind with an acceptable concept of belief. For Abram, the Word recorded:

> Genesis 15: 6 kjv 6 And he believed in the LORD, and he accounted it to him for righteousness.

The Committee also noted the changing interpretations due to a change in context. They noted that flesh was meat and there had been a difference that was specific between the flesh of animals and the flesh of mankind just as there was a major difference between the Levitical priesthood and the priesthood of Jesus as the Christ in the priesthood of Melchizedek (Hebrews 7 in the Word). (The Committee noted this hidden shadow often not discussed. Jesus was not a Levite and therefore His priesthood was of a different heredity through His virgin birth (not His physical heredity of mankind being from the tribe of Judah.)) Mankind was to note these differences as ages passed. Another context difference in the flesh as meat dealt with understanding of the Word according to an analogy presented by Paul under the inspiration of the Holy Spirit. Paul contrasted meat with milk as meat being a food representing greater strength in understanding of the Word and salvation plan when compared to a weaker understanding when being on the milk of the Word. The analogy simply compared a baby being on milk at first and then being able to feed on meat through growth. The Committee understood that mankind has the ability to understand these analogies as shadows of the spiritual truth. (If for some reason one of mankind has inefficient ability, the Committee recognizes the opportunity to provide ***mercy*** as a remedy.) Mankind has been provided the analogy between seen physical meat and use of the spiritual meat included in Paul's discussion to recognize the unseen realms. Note that there is a continuation of the two spiritual realms for mankind to decide between in the Committee's plan. Paul's discussion of meat in the New Testament is referring to mankind's realization of the substance in the Committee's attempt to show the decision needed for obeying the commandments set forth for the competition. The competition described in the beginning is now between the free will choice of mankind to accept Jesus or to accept Satan. Other food for thought to support the recognition of the unseen realms is provided by the chronological events revealed in the recordings of the Word and continue to be noted in the following discussions.

The following simple Word has a two-fold meaning. 1. The Word is true for the physical body. 2. The hidden portion became true for the spiritual body although the spiritual glorified body may not need the blood except to be shed by Jesus on the cross.

<sub>Leviticus 17:11 kjv 11</sub>For the life of the flesh is in the blood: and I have given it to you upon the altar to make

an atonement for your souls: for it is the blood that maketh an atonement for the soul.

**The Shadow of the feasts . . .** The plan included setting up seven prominent feasts (Four already discussed by the Committee and fulfilled by Jesus on the cross in death, burial, and resurrection.) to be held through the year. Each of these feasts provide hidden support relating future fulfillments that has been partially fulfilled. The fulfillments that have happened indicate the life of Christ as Jesus. As Jesus the plan was for Him as a spiritual being to transcend into the physical realm so the images then produced could see the unseen. This was a major and magnificent fulfillment for all to recognize. (The Committee noted in the present age it is sometimes hard to recognize how the present fits into a pattern. This is like looking at the irrigation circles in a field when on the ground and looking at the irrigation circles from an airplane. One cannot see the irrigation circles in their pattern on the ground since one may be too close on the ground which is a different frame to view from. Mankind often uses the saying that one cannot see the forest for the trees. This forms the same concept as in the air one can see from a different view.)

The Jewish rulers (priests) for the most part at the time of Christ (being visible as Jesus) focused on the physical Jesus and failed to accept Him and recognize His fulfilling of prophesy. The Committee's plan that involved the transition from not seeing to seeing abilities of the created mankind was to be fulfilled and understood by mankind more as time passed. (Again, it was noted that the Committee planned for mankind to understand prophesied events afterward as mankind looked back and recognized how it happened. The Committee noted the following example in the history of mankind. As Columbus sailed in a previous age, many were thinking the horizon might be the edge on a flat earth and he would drop off and it was afterward the earth was considered not to be flat. Thus again, the original view is misleading from what is seen to what is proven to be true. This is a representation of the ultimate plan as now discussed by the Committee (***in hopes the substance and evidence will help provide belief and faith as mankind uses ears to hear the Word so faith will come***) . . . to show the truth of what is unseen by the creation (mankind) and guide them into accepting the unseen that is not in the seen environment.)

> Romans 10:17 kjv 17So then faith cometh by hearing, and hearing by the word of God.

> Hebrews 11:6 kjv 6But without faith it is impossible to please him: for he that cometh to God must believe that he is, and that he is a rewarder of them that diligently seek him.

Now back to the feasts: Each of the feasts had a hidden meaning and the Committee could not have been more straight forward as the design was and is to make the patterns represented in the hidden messages to be more evident in a future time rather than in the past present time of the pharisees and the Sadducees.. The following procedure did have a true meaning until events in the future unfolded through the ages. With time meanings began to develop into truer meanings. Often in the Word

Jesus had given a more direct revelation of the hidden shadows. The Committee discussed the hidden meaning again of Jesus being the unleavened bread in symbolism. He had actually indicated this shadow as related to the Pharisees and Sadducees and is now recorded in the Word.

> Matthew 16:6 kjv 6 Then Jesus said unto them, Take heed and beware of the leaven of the Pharisees and of the Sadducees.

> Matthew 16:11-12 kjv 11 How is it that ye do not understand that I spake it not to you concerning bread, that ye should beware of the leaven of the Pharisees and of the Sadducees? Then understood they how that he bade them not beware of the leaven of bread, but of the doctrine of the Pharisees and of the Sadducees.

(The Committee noted also that the Word continued to indicate lack of immediate understanding by the apostles. Understanding was to come later.)

One of the feasts (Exodus 12 as previously discussed and now fulfilled) was set up to be performed as follows: (Note: This feast to be known as the Passover was one of the favorites for the Committee and had already been considered a shadow representation of Jesus as the true Lamb and now the emphasis was as the _Passover at the end times to be found in the Word (Revelations)._) A male lamb was to be taken by a family and selected so that is was as perfect as they could find. This lamb was to be put to death and the blood placed on the frame of the door. This was the time of the

Egyptian captivity of the developing descendants of Abraham into a nation. Moses was about to do the bidding of the Committee and provide a last plague on the Egyptians. The descendants of Abraham that performed this command to provide the lamb's blood on the door frame as requested were saved from the plague. (The Committee noted that the then present creation (mankind) that existed then thought of doing this out of faith in the unseen and saw it merely as a command from the Committee through Moses The Committee continued to use selected mankind to provide information from the unseen to the seen. However, the hidden plan was for the future ages to look back and see the pattern that Jesus provided as a representation of the true Lamb.)

The Committee noted the seven feasts are the Passover, Feast of Unleavened Bread, Feast of First Fruits, Pentecost (Shavuot}, Feast of Trumpets, Day of Atonement (Yom Kippur), and Feast of Tabernacles (Succoth). At this time, these latter three feasts are only partially fulfilled. The Committee mentioned briefly that Jesus came in His body as a tabernacle or temple and partially fulfilled the Feast of Tabernacles. Careful study in the Word would reveal that Jesus' birth was during the celebration of the Feast of Tabernacles and not in December of mankind's present calendar. Hence, Jesus came in his tabernacle at the time of the Feast of Tabernacle and was again signifying mankind to focus on the feasts.

The Committee again recalled the shadow of unleavened bread being the ONE prepared body and fulfilling the Passover feast. They also noted that the shadow of division in the tabernacle as the curtain represented mankind's flesh. This division being done away with by Jesus sacrificing his specially prepared body of flesh is recorded as an important recognition of the hidden meaning of the curtain as a shadow. This removal of flesh (the curtain) provided the indwelling of the Holy Spirit when and if individual mankind believed and accepted the redemption plan of the cross. This belief had to be and is of self's free will as Jesus had of His own free will submitted to the demand of Him being the flesh sacrificed on the cross. The Committee mentioned the true Lord's prayer in the Garden of Gethsemane as recorded in the Word (Matthew 26:36-46 kjv). The Committee also recalled that the Word had mentioned the shadow of bread representing Jesus' flesh.

> John 6:35 kjv 35 And Jesus said unto them, I am the bread of life: he that cometh to me shall never hunger; and he that believeth on me shall never thirst.

> John 6:51 kjv 51 I am the living bread which came down from heaven: if any man eat of this bread, he shall live for ever: and the bread that I will give is __my flesh__, which I will give for the life of the world.

(The flesh was of the ONE perfect body.)

**The Shadow of Elisha. and Elisha . . .** The hidden representations of the unseen to represent patterns that the Committee designed offers a challenge to mankind understanding hidden shadows as planned by the Committee. One of the planned hidden representations of the unseen future events discussed by the Committee was presented by the seen actions of Elisha and Elijah. Elisha became a definite follower of Elijah and went with him wherever he went. Elijah was to cross the Jordan river and on the other side Elijah was taken by the Committee without Elijah dying a physical death. Elijah told Elisha who wanted to go and went with Elijah in crossing the Jordan river that if Elisha saw Elijah go then Elisha would receive a double portion from the Committee of the power that the Committee had provided Elijah. Elisha crossed the Jordan with Elijah and saw him go into the heavenly (the unseen realm) and leave the earth (the seen realm). After that Elisha received a double portion of the power Elijah had. This sequence provided a wonderful hidden shadow although not explained but left for mankind to wonder about it. (The Committee had several shadows that was simply left for mankind to wonder about the true representation.) The Committee discussed this shadow and decided that mankind when studying the sequence of Elisha and Elijah both crossing the Jordan River, then Elijah stayed and was carried to heaven with Elisha going back across the Jordan with an increase in powers . . . Mankind might think of the Holy Spirit descending when Jesus the Christ ascended. After the fulfillment of Jesus and the Holy Spirit (the seen with the unseen) crossing from physical (seen) death into the heavenly (unseen) as in crossing the Jordan (crossing from the seen into the unseen) and afterward the (unseen) Holy Ghost returning across the boundary (Jordan river representation) with a lot more power from the Committee, the wonderful shadow should be understood. Elisha (a physical representation of the Comforter or Holy Spirit) and Elijah (a physical representation of the glorified body of Jesus as Christ) should be evident.

<sub>2 Kings 2:6-14 kjv</sub> 6 And Elijah said unto him, Tarry, I pray thee, here; for the LORD hath sent me to Jordan. And he said, As the LORD liveth, and as thy soul liveth, I will not leave thee. And they two went on. 7 And fifty men of the sons of the prophets went, and stood to view afar off: and they two stood by Jordan. 8 And Elijah took his mantle, and wrapped it together, and smote the waters, and they were divided hither and thither, so that they two went over on dry ground. 9 And it came to pass, when they were gone over, that Elijah said unto Elisha, Ask what I shall do for thee, before I be taken away from thee. And Elisha said, I pray thee, let a double portion of thy spirit be upon me. 10 And he said, Thou hast asked a hard thing: nevertheless, if thou see me when I am taken from thee, it shall be so unto thee; but if not, it shall not be so. 11 And it came to pass, as they still went on, and talked, that, behold, there appeared a chariot of fire, and horses of fire, and parted them both asunder; and Elijah went up by a whirlwind into heaven. 12 And Elisha saw it, and he cried, My father, my father, the chariot of Israel, and the horsemen thereof. And he saw him no more: and he took hold of his own clothes, and rent them in two pieces. 13 He took up also the mantle of Elijah that fell from him, and went back, and stood by the bank of Jordan; 14 And he took the mantle of Elijah that fell from him, and smote the waters, and said,

Where is the LORD God of Elijah? and when he also had smitten the waters, they parted hither and thither: and Elisha went over.

**The Shadow to Be Born Again:** In John chapter 3 an incident is given to Nicodemus, a ruler of the Jews where the rebirth (unseen) of individuals is presented by the speech of Jesus. As in the wind moving leaves (seen) provides effects supporting the existence of the wind (unseen) so the spiritual rebirth (unseen) of the individual provides evidence that supports the existence of the individual change in contrast to the physical birth (seen). The following scriptures provide a revelation of the hidden plan as provided through the Committee's recorded plan.

John 3:1-7 kjv ¹There was a man of the Pharisees, named Nicodemus, a ruler of the Jews: ²The same came to Jesus by night, and said unto him, Rabbi, we know that thou art a teacher come from God: for no man can do these miracles that thou doest, except God be with him. ³Jesus answered and said unto him, Verily, verily, I say unto thee, Except a man be born again, he cannot see the kingdom of God. ⁴Nicodemus saith unto him, How can a man be born when he is old? can he enter the second time into his mother's womb, and be born? ⁵Jesus answered, Verily, verily, I say unto thee, Except a man be born of water and of the Spirit, he cannot enter into the kingdom of God. ⁶That which is born of the flesh is flesh; and that which is born of the Spirit is spirit. ⁷Marvel not that I said unto thee, Ye must be born again.

***Where Did Jesus Go:*** When Jesus spoke, He often revealed far reaching revelations of the Committee's plan for future events. (Again, the Committee remembered Jesus stated the plan of the Committee to have told events of the future that would be fulfilled so that the special created individual images should understand how some events could happen in the future that could not have happened in the past. This was the intent of the many representations throughout the Word.) Jesus directly told the apostles where He was going in the sequence of death, burial, and resurrection. (This is what John came to realize and believe when Jesus moved out of the tomb.}

> John 14:1-4 kjv ¹Let not your heart be troubled: ye believe in God, believe also in me. ²In my Father's house are many mansions: if it were not so, I would have told you. I go to prepare a place for you. ³And if I go and prepare a place for you, I will come again, and receive you unto myself; that where I am, there ye may be also. ⁴And whither I go ye know, and the way ye know.

*The Revealing in Hebrews:* The Committee permitted the writer of Hebrews an insight into the hidden design of the seen service of the mankind priests and the physical temple to represent the Priest actions of Christ in representing the lamb as well as the high priest in the service. The Levitical priests carried out the redemptive service (physically . . . seen but hidden from individual views) within the tabernacle (temple). This was again planned so mankind would have another opportunity to view the true ultimate strategy to have the temple represent every one of the special created image (mankind) and the priestly actions in redemption to represent the work of the unseen Holy Ghost within mankind.

***The shadow of The Light of the World:*** Jesus declared Himself as the Light of the world. This statement contained a hidden clue that is continuing to unfold as mankind recognizes the meaning. An easy understanding is that the light represents mankind having a recognition and knowledge of new things including what is referred to as "opening the eyes." There is often a transition to "opening mankind's eyes" to see the previously unseen. A deeper study of light into scientific studies reveals that light seems to be the result of transferring from matter into energy. Thus, there is a boundary between matter and energy represented by light. Evidence of the unseen (ray of light) being a boundary between the seen (matter) as a representation of transition between the seen realm and the unseen realm becomes evident and becomes a revelation to mankind of the possible transition to come. This shadow of light is a great representation of the transition of the sinful physical body into the celestial body as the believed hope of all Christians.

> John 8:12 kjv 12Then spake Jesus again unto them, saying, I am the light of the world: he that followeth me shall not walk in darkness, but shall have the light of life.

John 1:1-14 kjv 1 In the beginning was the Word, and the Word was with God, and the Word was God. 2 The same was in the beginning with God. 3 All things were made by him; and without him was not anything made that was made. 4 In him was life; and the life was the light of men. 5 And the light shineth in darkness; and the darkness comprehended it not. 6 There was a man sent from God, whose name was John 7 The same came for a witness, to bear witness of the Light, that all men through him might believe. 8 He was not that Light, but was sent to bear witness of that Light. 9 That was the true Light, which lighteth every man that cometh into the world. 10 He was in the world, and the world was made by him, and the world knew him not. 11 He came unto his own, and his own received him not. 12 But as many as received him, to them gave the power to become the sons of God, even to them that believe on his name: 13 Which were born, not of blood, nor of the will of the flesh, nor of the will of man, but of God. 14 And the Word was made flesh, and dwelt among us, (and we beheld his glory, the glory as of the only begotten of the Father,) full of grace and truth.

*The Teaching by Jesus:* The Committee mentioned the hidden light provided in the teaching of Jesus. The teaching by Jesus involves at least two presentations to mankind of the transition of the seen toward the unseen. His actual actions fulfilled the scriptures that foretold many facets of his actual physical life to be seen. Also, his teaching often provided hidden meanings that could be interpreted by mankind. Some of these teaching events resulted in what mankind calls parables. Many parables represent the hidden view of the redemptive plan of the Committee.

*The Suffering Servant*: During the Old Testament one finds many hidden representations of the Committee's plan. Some were meant to be puzzling until they were fulfilled. (Remember the words of Jesus in John about telling what was to happen so that the apostles might understand.) One of the puzzling prophecies was that the Messiah (Jesus) was to be a suffering individual. The puzzling event became real and understandable when Jesus made the transition through the Cross (death, burial, new birth, and resurrection) in a seen bodily resurrection as a suffering servant into the unseen realm to become a king descending from David through Mary being the mother. Jesus was the seen suffering servant and is now planned to become the king. As continued to be the basic plan for mankind if they believed, the virgin birth (recorded in Isaiah) fulfilled the needed perfect sacrifice in not having an Adamic sin. The Committee again considered the woman (Eve) broke a commandment of the Committee through temptation while Adam of his own free will committed the Adamic sin. The Committee wanted this sin to be viewed by mankind as viewed by the Committee. The free will decision was, is and continues to be a major part of accepting and following the commandments of the Committee. This is a truth throughout the recorded history (recorded in the

Word). The suffering savior had been recorded in the Word as already indicated.

> Isaiah 53:1-12 kjv ¹Who hath believed our report? and to whom is the arm of the LORD revealed? ²For he shall grow up before him as a tender plant, and as a root out of a dry ground: he hath no form nor comeliness; and when we shall see him, there is no beauty that we should desire him. ³He is despised and rejected of men; a man of sorrows, and acquainted with grief: and we hid as it were our faces from him; he was despised, and we esteemed him not. ⁴Surely he hath borne our griefs, and carried our sorrows: yet we did esteem him stricken, smitten of God, and afflicted. ⁵But he was wounded for our transgressions, he was bruised for our iniquities: the chastisement of our peace was upon him; and with his stripes we are healed. ⁶All we like sheep have gone astray; we have turned every one to his own way; and the LORD hath laid on him the iniquity of us all. ⁷He was oppressed, and he was afflicted, yet he opened not his mouth: he is brought as a lamb to the slaughter, and as a sheep before her shearers is dumb, so he openeth not his mouth. ⁸He was taken from prison and from judgment: and who shall declare his generation? for he was cut off out of the land of the living: for the transgression of my people was he stricken. ⁹And he made his grave with the wicked, and with the rich in his death; because he had done no violence, neither was any deceit in his mouth. ¹⁰Yet it pleased the LORD to

bruise him; he hath put him to grief: when thou shalt make his soul an offering for sin, he shall see his seed, he shall prolong his days, and the pleasure of the LORD shall prosper in his hand. ¹¹He shall see of the travail of his soul, and shall be satisfied: by his knowledge shall my righteous servant justify many; for he shall bear their iniquities. ¹²Therefore will I divide him a portion with the great, and he shall divide the spoil with the strong; because he hath poured out his soul unto death: and he was numbered with the transgressors; and he bare the sin of many, and made intercession for the transgressors.

*Jesus as the Word*: As found in John 1 . . . Events are continuing to fulfill the prediction of Jesus as the Savior and reveal to mankind as expected and planned by the Committee. The hidden portion of the plan was understood it seems by John who begin to understand what was happening at the then present time of Jesus' glorified body being seen in presentations. This was directly revealed by the Committee through John's writing in John chapter 1. The written Word is now seen to be the living Word in Jesus. (The Committee was and is completely satisfied with the planned result of the past, the present result, and the coming future results for mankind.)

John 1:1-14 kjv ¹In the beginning was the Word, and the Word was with God, and the Word was God. ²The same was in the beginning with God. ³All things were made by him; and without him was not any thing made that was made. ⁴In him was life; and the life was the light of men. [5]And the light shineth in darkness; and the darkness comprehended it not. [6]There was a man sent from God, whose name was John. [7]The same came for a witness, to bear witness of the Light, that all men through him might believe. [8]He was not that Light, but was sent to bear witness of that Light. [9]That was the true Light, which lighteth every man that cometh into the world. [10]He was in the world, and the world was made by him, and the world knew him not. [11]He came unto his own, and his own received him not. [12]But as many as received him, to them gave he power to become the sons of God, even to them that believe on his name: [13]Which were born, not of blood, nor of the will of the flesh, nor of the will of man, but of God. [14]And the Word was made flesh, and dwelt among us, (and we beheld his glory, the glory as of the only begotten of the Father,) full of grace and truth.

## Chapter IV

### *The Transition Period . . . From Peter to Paul*

The Committee noted this transition period as Phase I in their great plan and at this meeting they recognized it as being in the past planning and now in the present. The prophecy period had ended and now the mystery period had become known. In brief summary, Israel had now been blinded and the mystery period was to let the gentiles have the same opportunity to spread the light out of the darkness. The Committee now reviewed the transition from Peter to Paul. The Committee in review included a summary of previously discussed items in the Word.

The Committee rehearsed the major use of prophesy to set up the fulfillment of the kingdom and the transition of the mystery to complete the future plan for all mankind. The Committee discussed the gaps found in prophecy that mankind needed to understand. A gap was a division in the seventy-year prophecy given to Daniel and relayed to mankind. A major gap hidden was between the first sixty-nine years and the last week of years. A hidden gap had depended on the self-will reception of Jesus as the true Messiah of Israel through the Israelite leaders and most Israelites. At the time of Jesus, the Israelites through their leaders had crucified Jesus and brought condemnation upon the Israelite nation (although a remnant had believed in Jesus.)

> <sup>Matthew 27:22-25 kjv</sup> ²²Pilate saith unto them, What shall I do then with Jesus which is called Christ? They all say unto him, Let him be crucified. ²³And the governor said, Why, what evil hath he done? But they cried out the more, saying, Let him be crucified. ²⁴When Pilate saw that he could prevail nothing, but that rather a tumult was made, he took water, and washed his hands before the multitude, saying, I am innocent of the blood of this just person: see ye to it. ²⁵<u>Then answered all the people, and said, His blood be on us, and on our children.</u>

The Committee noted an item of knowledge . . . that belief does not necessarily mean understanding. They recalled the Committee's inspired teaching by Paul to pastors and individual mankind to rightly divide the Word of truth. They discussed the dividing of the Word represented by the teaching of the coming kingdom by the apostles in prophecy <u>since the world began</u> and the mystery body of Christ as taught by Paul and <u>kept secret since the world began</u>. This was a major division known in the Word as being between prophecy of the nations and Jesus and the mystery gap. Many mankind have now come to recognize this gap as resulting because of the rejection of Jesus by the Israelites. This opened up the mystery period of time to be revealed.

2 Peter 1:21 kjv 21For the prophecy came not in old time by the will of man: but holy men of God spake as they were moved by the Holy Ghost.

Acts 3:21 kjv 21Whom the heaven must receive until the times of restitution of all things, which God hath spoken by the mouth of all his holy prophets *since the world began*.

Romans 16:25-27 kjv 25Now to him that is of power to stablish you according to my gospel, and the preaching of Jesus Christ, according to the revelation of the mystery, which *was kept secret since the world began*, 26But now is made manifest, and by the scriptures of the prophets, according to the commandment of the everlasting God, made known to all nations for the obedience of faith: 27To God only wise, be glory through Jesus Christ for ever. Amen.

(NOTE: The Committee discussed the important division they had placed in the Word. In Acts 3:21 the prophecies were ***given since the world began*** while in Romans 16 the hidden mystery was ***kept secret since the world began.*** This division is a major division of the truth for mankind to discern and understand as time passed and plans changed. This transition time is to be discussed briefly by the Committee before discussing in more detail the time of mystery.)

The Committee considered this the time of great fulfillment. The Passover feast had been set symbolically during the time of creating the nation of Israel in coming out of the four hundred years in the nation of Egypt. The Passover was a time of Jesus' fulfillment in being the true lamb of sacrifice. The fulfillment of the cross set in motion a hidden part of the Committee's plan. The Word recorded major portions of this transition period that has been a major accomplishment of the plan.

**At the cross:** The death of Jesus as the lamb of sacrifice set in motion major events that happened during the next three days. The veil petition between the earthly and the heavenly had been torn and opened. Jesus had taken the pure blood into the heavenly and completed the cleaning of the heavenly. Jesus took on His glorified body. A major use of power from the combination of the Committee through the Father had resulted in the transition to create the first glorified body. The glorified body was the first to have overcome a physical death to never die a physical death again but to have eternal life. With power the glorified Jesus as the first fruit traveled to paradise and the saints there took on glorified bodies through being a part of the first fruits. Paradise was moved to the heavenly position and the heavenly place (now clean) received paradise.

Jesus then verified his resurrection by appearing to the apostles and others during the next forty days. He appeared in his glorified body and demonstrated several characteristics of the new glorified body that were different from that of his physical body but also demonstrated some characteristics that seemed to have remained the same. After this period of forty days, the Son of the Father ascended to His position at the right hand of the Father as recorded in the Word. There He awaited to the time of Pentecost when the Holy Spirit took His position as the Comforter promised by Jesus.

A major goal of the apostles during this time between the cross and the coming of the Comforter for the apostles and Jews was a continued teaching of Jesus. They focused on teaching the Israelites as Jesus had directed them. They were looking for a quick return of the Messiah to set up His earthly kingdom. They knew He had told the apostles to go only to the "lost sheep of Israel" so this is what they did. In His glorified body Jesus had told Peter to go feed His sheep.

> John 21:14-16 kjv [14]This is now the third time that Jesus shewed himself to his disciples, after that he was risen from the dead. [15]So when they had dined, Jesus saith to Simon Peter, Simon, son of Jonas, lovest thou me more than these? He saith unto him, Yea, Lord; thou knowest that I love thee. He saith unto him, Feed my lambs. [16]He saith to him again the second time, Simon, son of Jonas, lovest thou me? He saith unto him, Yea, Lord; thou knowest that I love thee. He saith unto him, Feed my sheep. [17]He saith unto him the third time, Simon, son of Jonas, lovest thou me? Peter was grieved because he said unto him the third time, Lovest thou me? And he said unto him, Lord, thou knowest all things; thou knowest that I love thee. Jesus saith unto him, Feed my sheep.

The Holy Spirit taking position as planned during Pentecost completed the major set up as planned by the Committee. Earlier ages before the cross the Word recorded history foretold to create shadows to verify the existence of the unseen Committee and the truth about Jesus coming as the Messiah. The virgin birth through to the cross including the ascension has now placed the Father and the Son in their respective positions. The Comforter (Holy Spirit) has now also taken the position for His work in sealing those that believe and make the desired connection through the veil of flesh. The circumcision of the heart as the second covenant sealing foretold by Jeremiah 31:31 in the Word has now happened to true believers including gentiles as well as Israelites who have accepted the work of Jesus on the cross.

The final rejection by the Jews in the stoning of Stephen and recorded in the Word ushered in the hidden gap period to be known as the mystery age of grace. (The Committee briefly discussed the Word presentation by Stephen in Acts 7:2-53 as being one of the best summaries about relevant history of Israel for mankind to review and know and understand.) The result of Stephen rehearsing this history was the stoning and killing of Stephen.

> Acts 7:54-60 kjv 54When they heard these things, they were cut to the heart, and they gnashed on him with their teeth. 55But he, being full of the Holy Ghost, looked up stedfastly into heaven, and saw the glory of God, and Jesus standing on the right hand of God, 56And said, Behold, I see the heavens opened, and the Son of man standing on the right hand of God. 57Then they cried out with a loud voice, and stopped their ears, and ran upon him with one accord, 58And cast him out of the city, and stoned him: and the witnesses laid down their clothes at a young man's feet, whose name was Saul. 59And they stoned Stephen, calling upon God, and saying, Lord Jesus, receive my

spirit. ⁶⁰And he kneeled down, and cried with a loud voice, Lord, lay not this sin to their charge. And when he had said this, he fell asleep.

Scriptures related to the transition period between the cross and the Comforter were discussed as being provided for mankind to study and understand. (The Committee briefly discussed the hidden interesting fact that most mankind had missed. Most mankind thought that Israel had rejected Jesus and had failed to distribute the Word as the Committee had planned. Actually, the Committee through foreknowledge knew that rejection was the free will action to be made by the Jews. Therefore, the Committee let all of the books of the Word be written by Jews. Thus, the Israelites spread the Word when the Word was spread even though the Israelite nation had rejected Jesus. The Committee discussed their planning to use the Israelite rejection to fulfill the need for the cross and crucifixion in order to bring in the mystery age. The Committee had fulfilled (even though hidden) that the Israelites would indirectly spread the Word.)

The Committee was well pleased as each took planned positions. Symbolism in prophecy and other facets of the Word provided shadows that hid many items. The Word of Isaiah below indicated the inheritance of the Gentiles to take place. The Committee in discussing this passage of the Word found in Isaiah noted that it still referred to the coming seventieth week of Daniel. Interpretation provided by the Committee included using and reviewing chapter 12 of Revelations in the Word. In chapter 12 Israel represented as the mother had travailed in having Jesus as a child in the virgin birth. The barren that did not bear is the gentiles also known as the desolate. The married wife is represented as Israel with the husband as the Lord.

> Isaiah 54 kjv ¹Sing, O barren, thou that didst not bear; break forth into singing, and cry aloud, thou that didst not travail with child: for more are the children of the desolate than the children of the **married wife**, saith the LORD. ²Enlarge the place of thy tent, and let them stretch forth the curtains of thine habitations: spare not, lengthen thy cords, and strengthen thy stakes; ³For thou shalt break forth on the right hand and on the left; and <u>*thy seed*</u> shall inherit the Gentiles, and make the desolate cities to be inhabited. ⁴Fear not; for thou shalt not be ashamed: neither be thou confounded; for thou shalt not be put to shame: for thou shalt forget the shame of thy youth, and shalt not remember the reproach of thy widowhood any more. ⁵**For thy Maker is thine husband**; the LORD of hosts is his name; and thy Redeemer the Holy One of Israel; The God of the whole earth shall he be called. ⁶For the LORD hath called thee as a woman forsaken and grieved in spirit, and a wife of youth, when thou wast refused, saith thy God. ⁷For a small moment have I forsaken thee; but with great mercies will I gather thee. ⁸In a little wrath I hid my face from thee for a moment; but with everlasting kindness will I have mercy on thee, saith the LORD thy redeemer. ⁹For this is as <u>*the waters of Noah unto me: for as I have sworn that the waters of Noah should no more go over the*</u>

*earth; so have I sworn that I would not be wroth with thee, nor rebuke thee.* ¹⁰For the mountains shall depart, and the hills be removed; but my kindness shall not depart from thee, neither shall the covenant of my peace be removed, saith the LORD that hath mercy on thee. ¹¹O thou afflicted, tossed with tempest, and not comforted, behold, I will lay thy stones with fair colours, and lay thy foundations with sapphires. ¹²And I will make thy windows of agates, and thy gates of carbuncles, and all thy borders of pleasant stones. ¹³And all thy children shall be taught of the LORD; and great shall be the peace of thy children. ¹⁴In righteousness shalt thou be established: thou shalt be far from oppression; for thou shalt not fear: and from terror; for it shall not come near thee. ¹⁵Behold, they shall surely gather together, but not by me: whosoever shall gather together against thee shall fall for thy sake. ¹⁶Behold, I have created the smith that bloweth the coals in the fire, and that bringeth forth an instrument for his work; and I have created the waster to destroy. ¹⁷No weapon that is formed against thee shall prosper; and every tongue that shall rise against thee in judgment thou shalt condemn. This is the heritage of the servants of the LORD, and their righteousness is of me, saith the LORD.

**The First Fruits:** Matthew 27:50-53 kjv ⁵⁰Jesus, when he had cried again with a loud voice, yielded up the ghost. ⁵¹And, behold, the veil of the temple was rent in twain from the top to the bottom; and the earth did quake, and the rocks rent; ⁵²And the graves were opened; and many bodies of the saints which slept arose, ⁵³And came out of the graves *after his resurrection*, and went into the holy city, and appeared unto many.

Hebrews 10:20 kjv ²⁰By a new and living way, which he hath consecrated for us, through the veil, that is to say, his flesh;

Romans 8:29 kjv ²⁹For whom he did foreknow, he also did predestinate to be conformed to the image of his Son, that he might be the firstborn among many brethren.

The Committee remembered that removing the veil removed the separation of the most holy from the holy represented in the tabernacle shadow. This signified the separation between God and mankind that had resulted because of the Adamic sin in the Garden of Eden. This removal of the curtain was a shadow of letting the most holy associate with mankind with forgiveness of sin for the first time since in the garden. Understanding that the curtain represented the desires of the flesh of mankind included letting the Holy Spirit take a powerful position in entering into mankind. This mystery still remains today. The reunion was also a mystery not yet completely revealed and explained although presented in the ministry inspired through Paul. However, faith and belief were and are still the keys to the glory passing through the veil (flesh). Again, the Committee noted that faith and belief did not mean understanding of details through complete knowledge. Faith and believing for mankind depended on acknowledgement of the unseen realm of the Committee by seen results. Seen results due to fulfilled prophecy had been the plan of the Committee. The Committee remembered again that Jesus had stated the plan in the Word by emphasizing telling events ahead of time so that when the events came to pass mankind should believe by seeing in their mind's eye.

> 2 Corinthians 3:13-16 kjv 13 And not as Moses, which put a veil over his face, that the <u>children of Israel could not stedfastly look to the end of that which is abolished:</u> 14 *But their minds* were blinded: for until this day remaineth the same vail untaken away in the reading of the old testament; which vail is done away in Christ. 15 But even unto this day, when Moses is read, <u>the vail is upon their heart.</u> 16 Nevertheless when it shall turn to the Lord, the vail shall be taken away.

Paul had now been given supporting background for teaching in the mystery age. This was different from what the apostles had been teaching. Peter indicated the difficulty in understanding the shadows being applied to the age of mystery.

> 2 Peter 3:16 kjv 16 As also in all his epistles, speaking in them of these things; in which are some things **hard to** be understood, which they that are unlearned and unstable wrest, as they do also the other scriptures, unto their own destruction.

The Committee recalled about how they had summarized the redemptive plan as it had been presented in the Word

169

plainly for mankind to understand and respond to. The Committee reviewed the excellent summary of the basis for the redemptive plan needed to be understood by mankind. This involved the change in the covenants from circumcision of the flesh and to circumcision of the heart (including determination of free will set through appropriate faith and belief).

Hebrews 9:1-28 kjv 1 Then verily the first covenant had also ordinances of divine service, and a worldly sanctuary. 2 For there was a tabernacle made; the first, wherein was the candlestick, and the table, and the shewbread; which is called the sanctuary. 3 And after the second veil, the tabernacle which is called the Holiest of all; 4 Which had the golden censer, and the ark of the covenant overlaid round about with gold, wherein was the golden pot that had manna, and Aaron's rod that budded, and the tables of the covenant; 5 And over it the cherubims of glory shadowing the mercyseat; of which we cannot now speak particularly. 6 Now when these things were thus ordained, the priests went always into the first tabernacle, accomplishing the service of God. 7 But into the second went the high priest alone once every year, not without blood, which he offered for himself, and for the errors of the people: 8 The Holy Ghost this signifying, that the way into the holiest of all was not yet made manifest, while as the first tabernacle was yet standing: 9 Which was a figure for the time then present, in which were offered both gifts and sacrifices, that could not make him that did the service perfect, as pertaining to the conscience; ¹⁰Which stood only in meats and drinks, and divers washings, and carnal ordinances, imposed on them until the time of reformation. ¹¹But Christ being come an high priest of good things to come, by a greater and more perfect tabernacle, not made with hands, that is to say, not of this building; ¹²Neither by the blood of goats and calves, but by his own blood he entered in once into the holy place, having obtained eternal redemption for us. ¹³For if the blood of bulls and of goats, and the ashes of an heifer sprinkling the unclean, sanctifieth to the purifying of the flesh: ¹⁴How much more shall the blood of Christ, who through the eternal Spirit offered himself without spot to God, purge your conscience from dead works to serve the living God? ¹⁵And for this cause he is the mediator of the new testament, that by means of death, for the redemption of the transgressions that were under the first testament, they which are called might receive the promise of eternal inheritance. ¹⁶For where a testament is, there must also of necessity be the death of the testator. ¹⁷For a testament is of force after men are dead: otherwise it is of no strength at all while the testator liveth. ¹⁸Whereupon neither the first testament was dedicated without blood. ¹⁹For when Moses had spoken every precept to all the people according to the law, he took the blood of calves and of goats, with water, and scarlet wool, and hyssop, and sprinkled both the book, and all the people, ²⁰ Saying, This is the blood of the testament which God hath enjoined unto you. ²¹ Moreover he sprinkled with blood both the tabernacle, and all the vessels of the ministry. ²² And almost all things are by the law purged with blood; and without shedding of blood is no remission. *²³ It was therefore necessary that the patterns of things in the heavens should be purified with these; but the heavenly things themselves with better sacrifices than these. ²⁴ For Christ is not entered into the holy places made with hands, which are the figures of the true; but into heaven itself, now to appear in the presence of God for us: ²⁵ Nor yet that he should offer himself often, as the high priest entereth into the holy place every year with blood of others; ²⁶ For then must he often have suffered since the foundation of the world: but now once in the end of the world hath he appeared to put away sin by the sacrifice of himself.* ²⁷ And as it is appointed unto men once to die, but after this the judgment: ²⁸ So Christ was once offered to bear the sins of many; and unto them that look for him shall he appear the second time without sin unto salvation.

Hebrews 10:1-39 kjv ¹For the law having a *shadow* of good things to come, and not the very image of the things, can never with those sacrifices which they offered year by year continually make the comers thereunto perfect. ²For then would they not have ceased to be offered? because that the worshippers once purged should have had no more conscience of sins ³But in those sacrifices there is a remembrance again made of sins every year. ⁴For it is not possible that the blood of bulls and of goats should take away sins. ⁵Wherefore *when he cometh into the world, he saith, Sacrifice and offering thou wouldest not, but a **body** hast thou prepared me:* ⁶In burnt offerings and sacrifices for sin thou hast had no pleasure. ⁷Then said I, Lo, I come (in the volume of the book it is written of me,) to do thy will, O God. ⁸Above when he said, Sacrifice and offering and burnt offerings and offering for sin thou wouldest not, neither hadst pleasure therein; which are offered by the law; ⁹Then said he, Lo, I come to do thy will, O God. He taketh away the first, that he may establish the second. ¹⁰By the which will we are sanctified through the *offering of the **body** of Jesus Christ once for all*. ¹¹And every priest standeth daily ministering and offering oftentimes the same sacrifices, which can never take away sins: ¹²But this man, after he had offered one sacrifice for sins for ever, sat down on the right hand of God; ¹³From henceforth expecting till his enemies be made his footstool. ¹⁴For by one offering he hath perfected for ever them that are sanctified. ¹⁵Whereof the Holy Ghost also is a witness to us: for after that he had said before, ¹⁶This is the covenant that I will make with them after those days, saith the Lord, I will put my laws *into their hearts, and in their minds* will I write them; ¹⁷And their sins and iniquities will I remember no more. ¹⁸Now where remission of these is, there *is no more offering for sin.* ¹⁹Having therefore, brethren, boldness to enter into the holiest by the blood of Jesus, ²⁰By a new and living way, which he hath consecrated for us, *through the veil, that is to say, his flesh;* ²¹And having an high priest over the house of God; ²²Let us draw near with a true heart in full assurance of faith, having our hearts sprinkled from an evil conscience, and our bodies washed with pure water. ²³Let us hold fast the profession of our faith without wavering; (for he is faithful that promised;) ²⁴And let us consider one another to provoke unto love and to good works: ²⁵Not forsaking the assembling of ourselves together, as the manner of some is; but exhorting one another: and so much the more, as ye see the day approaching. ²⁶For if we sin wilfully after that we have received the knowledge of the truth, there remaineth no more sacrifice for sins, ²⁷But a certain fearful looking for of judgment and fiery indignation, which shall devour the adversaries. ²⁸He that despised Moses' law died without mercy under two or three witnesses: ²⁹Of how much sorer punishment, suppose ye, shall he be thought worthy, who hath trodden under foot the Son of God, and hath counted the blood of the covenant, wherewith he was sanctified, an unholy thing, and hath done despite unto the Spirit of grace? ³⁰For we know him that hath said, Vengeance belongeth unto me, I will recompense, saith the Lord. And again, The Lord shall judge his people. ³¹It is a fearful thing to fall into the hands of the living God. ³²But call to remembrance the former days, in which, after ye were illuminated, ye endured a great fight of afflictions; ³³Partly, whilst ye were made a gazingstock both by reproaches and afflictions; and partly, whilst ye became companions of them that were so used. ³⁴For ye had compassion of me in my bonds, and took joyfully the spoiling of your goods, knowing in yourselves that ye have in heaven a better and an enduring substance. ³⁵Cast not away therefore your confidence, which hath great recompence of reward. ³⁶For ye have need of patience, that, after ye have done the will of God, ye might receive the promise. ³⁷For yet a little while, and he that shall come will come, and will not tarry. ³⁸Now the just shall live by faith: but if any man draw back, my soul shall have no pleasure in him. ³⁹But we are not of them who draw back unto perdition; but of them that believe to the saving of the soul.

The Committee was now ready to look at Phase II in their great and mystery plan. The plan now reversed itself for mankind to recognize the BIG true TRUTH that had been hidden since the foundation of the world and to become known in revelation to be the LIVING WORD!! The "I AM" as Jesus was and is the mystery revealed today. John, Ch. 1 in the Written Word records this major truth as discussed previously in this meeting.

## Chapter V

### Truth 3 Phase II: Mysteries Revealed . . .

### Chapter V Truth 3: The mystery: Now revealed (Why kept as a mystery?)

**Brief Summary:** *The Committee now noted that mankind up to the end of phase I of their plan had used their individual free will with the majority following and allowing Satan to control the ruling government of the Israelites. The individuals that had allowed this had not been in the true light. Thus, Phase II involves a change from Peter to Paul and involves the longsuffering and mercy of the Committee. This change involved and now is the revealed hidden mystery of the final opportunity for ALL mankind to be successful as recorded in the WORD and explained through the mystery as PHASE II of the TRUTH!!*

The seventy-week prophecy given to Daniel focuses on the sequence of Israel history along with the relation to other nations. The history of the Jews (representing all tribes of the Israelites) is followed in the Word with the seventy-week prophecy (490 years). Sixty-nine years had passed when the Committee suddenly revealed a hidden time gap in their plan. This hidden gap of time had been planned to be inserted between the sixty-ninth week of Daniel's prophecy and the seventieth week. The apostles were assigned by Jesus to stick to the prophecy of the coming kingdom for Israel and other nations on earth. Paul was the one chosen to present the hidden period of time focusing on the gentiles (but also including the Israelites that became unblinded to what Jesus had accomplished on the cross.) Note that Paul himself was a symbol of a blinded Jew that became unblinded on the road to Damascus in the physical representation of the spiritual phenomena.

Timeline without the mystery gap as expected by the Israelites and believers before the cross.

☐==============(Daniel)===========Jesus as messiah==Kingdom set up=☐

Timeline Surprise . . . death of Jesus not expected . . . end of 69th wk. . . . (mystery gap . . . ), 70th wk. . . . Resulting in the following unexpected timeline.

☐=(Jesus, cross, end of 69th wk.)===(mystery gap)(wk. 70)===Kingdom set up=☐

**<u>The Division of The Truth:</u>** The Committee rehearsed the major use of prophesy to set up the fulfillment of the kingdom and the mystery to complete the future plan for all mankind. They recalled the Committee's inspired teaching of Paul to pastors and individual mankind to rightly divide the Word of truth. They discussed the dividing of the Word represented by the teaching of the coming kingdom by the apostles and the mystery body of Christ as taught by Paul.

> <sub>2 Peter 1:21 kjv 21</sub>For the prophecy came not in old time by the will of man: but holy men of God spake as they were moved by the Holy Ghost.
> <sub>Acts 3:21 kjv 21</sub>Whom the heaven must receive until the times of restitution of all things, which God hath spoken by the mouth of all his holy prophets <u>since the world began</u>.
> <sub>Romans 16:25-27 kjv 25</sub>Now to him that is of power to stablish you according to my gospel, and the preaching of Jesus Christ, according to the revelation of the mystery, which <u>was kept secret since the world began</u>, <sup>26</sup>But now is made manifest, and by the scriptures of the prophets, according to the commandment of the everlasting God, made known to all nations for the obedience of faith: <sup>27</sup>To God only wise, be glory through Jesus Christ for ever. Amen.

**<u>The Shadows of Noah's Ark:</u>** Mankind now has the opportunity of hearing and reading the Committee's inspired accounts of appropriate interpretations of the shadows they have just discussed. Recorded information has been available to inspire many of mankind since the destruction of the physical temple in 70 A.D. along with present interpretations of the written Word. These interpretations if inspired by the Committee provides current opportunities to learn of the Committee. (An important comment discussed among the Committee was a need by mankind to always compare the true Word with mankind written interpretations. This was because of the opponent's (Satan) continued use of every opportunity possible to imitate and offer a fake alternative to mislead mankind away from the truth.) Many of the truly inspired current revelations had now become reported due to being a part of the increased ability to understand. New technology made events currently possible that could not have happened in earlier time ages. The Committee warned about mankind's responsibility to take care in making sure the interpretations reported were truly in concurrence with the recorded truth of the original Word.

> Revelation 22:18-19 kjv 18 For I testify unto every man that heareth the words of the prophecy of this book, If any man shall add unto these things, God shall add unto him the plagues that are written in this book: 19 And if any man shall take away from the words of the book of this prophecy, God shall take away his part out of the book of life, and out of the holy city, and from the things which are written in this book.

The Committee now turned to the Truth according to their overall plan for mankind and the recorded Word. As previously discussed, Paul had recorded in his pastoral writing to Timothy to correctly divide the Word of Truth. The Committee noted that most of mankind seemed to have missed this guide in study of the Word. The Committee discussed that mankind still did not in general correctly divide the Word as the Committee moved into consideration of the present age. The age of mystery introduced by Paul had now become the age of present time. Some of mankind had considered and did currently consider the Word as a guide for dividing the truth from the false. This reasoning seemed to be mainly based on the early stressing of the law and the ten commandments specifically. This early teaching to the very young and youth was planned to develop a base belief that should mature into more advanced truth as mankind grew older. As the Committee was now stressing in this meeting report, a major division in the Truth was the prophetic Word of truth focusing on Israel in the first covenant of Genesis 12 and the truth of the mysterious time (to now be discussed as the present age) gap focusing on the gentiles in the new covenant of Jeremiah 31:31-34 being now a possibility for believing gentiles also. The Committee considered that most of mankind had continued to "miss the boat" as a great number had missed the ark in Noah's time. This warning had been recorded in the Word as indicated below. The Committee considered Jesus' teaching where He had discussed the time of Noah in relation to the present and future situations of mankind in the world. (Some details related to the shadow of Noah's ark are to be discussed by the Committee later and also presented by inspired teachers and preachers of the Word during the current age.)

> Matthew 24:37 kjv 37But as the days of **Noah** were, so shall also the coming of the Son of man be.
>
> Luke 17:27 kjv 27They did eat, they drank, they married wives, they were given in marriage, until the day that **Noah** entered into the ark, and the flood came, and destroyed them all.
>
> Hebrews 11:7 kjv 7By faith **Noah**, being warned of God of things not seen as yet, moved with fear, prepared

an ark to the saving of his house; by the which he condemned the world, and became heir of the righteousness which is by faith.

<sub>1 Peter 3:20 kjv 20</sub>Which sometime were disobedient, when once the longsuffering of God waited in the days of **Noah**, while the ark was a preparing, wherein few, that is, eight souls were saved by water.

<sub>2 Peter 2:5 kjv 5</sub>And spared not the old world, but saved **Noah** the eighth person, a preacher of righteousness, bringing in the flood upon the world of the ungodly;

The Committee briefly discussed the symbolism of the ark built by Noah and the end time opportunity (including the present mystery age) to enter into the ark of safety provided by the current redemption plan. Inspired discussion of this symbolism has been available to mankind. Among these is a notable indication that the Committee had shut the door to the ark and Noah had no opportunity to let others into the ark once the door was shut.

<sub>Genesis 7:15-16 kjv 15</sub>And they went in unto Noah into the ark, two and two of all flesh, wherein is the breath of life. <sub>16</sub>And they that went in, went in male and female of all flesh, as God had commanded him: *and the LORD shut him in.*

**<u>The Original Plan:</u>** The reason for the two-fold division of the truth became a part of the plan based on the foreknowledge of the Committee along with their responsibility to maintain the truth of their unconditional covenants recorded in the Word. The first covenant should have had a result of the Israelite nation becoming a leader in spreading the great Commission of the Word to the rest of the Nations (mankind) in the time period following the cross to the time of Stephen's death. This was prior to the beginning of the mystery age. Free will entered in as most of the Israelites rejected Jesus as the messiah as provided in the prophetic Word. (Note that this rejection by most of Israelites at the time of Jesus' earthly ministry did not nullify the unconditional Abrahamic covenant for that era. That unconditional covenant is still in effect and will be fulfilled as the Committee continues into the fulfillment of the seventieth week of Daniel's prophecy. The Committee discussed their plan to place a mystery gap of time into the ages of time to provide all mankind with an opportunity to have sins forgiven by covering with the righteous blood of Jesus. (By foreknowledge, the Committee had planned the method to provide the true sinless sacrifice for remission of mankind's individual sins. The exchange of Jesus' righteousness for remission of mankind's sins is still a mystery for many. The Committee noted that the cross did not do away with mankind's sins but provided a method of remission.)

> Matthew 26:28 kjv 28 For this is my blood of the new testament, which is shed for many for the remission of sins.

> John 3:16 kjv 16 For God so loved the world, that he gave his only begotten Son, that whosoever believeth in him should not perish, but have everlasting life.

***The Mystery Age of Grace:*** The mystery age now became a major revelation as a division of truth hidden from the beginning of the world. The time gap now revealed had been hidden from not only all mankind but also from Satan and the fallen angels (demons). Thus, this surprise was a major victory in the plan of the Committee.

> I Corinthians 2:8 kjv 8 Which none of the princes of this world knew: for had they **known** it, they would **not** have crucified the Lord of glory.

The Committee now turned to a more detailed discussion of the mystery prepared for a surprise to all. Their foreknowledge had let the Committee to know that the Israelites would reject Jesus as the true Messiah of their own free will decision as the Committee had already discussed in the transition period comments. Thus, Israel missed the opportunity to accept Jesus as the king and set up the kingdom at the time of His earthly ministry **after** the cross and following Pentecost. (The Committee noted that this missed opportunity was like the new nation of Israel leaving the Egyptian captivity and coming to the boundary of their promised land. The new nation did not get to enter because of unbelief at that time also. The Committee mentioned this as a shadow repeated by Israel and by the gentiles so far.) (Jesus had to come as the Lamb in the first sixty-nine weeks to provide the suffering fulfillment of prophecy to get the perfect sacrifice needed for ALL and then would come the seventieth week of Daniel. The actual opportunity for the nation of Israel in general to accept Jesus as their Messiah came when His disciples preached following Pentecost.)  However, foreknowledge on the part of the Committee had indicated need for the plan as designed by the Committee. Therefore, the Committee had planned on Jesus coming as the Lamb and provide the method to forgive sin through the belief system. Mankind sinning was not gotten rid of, but individual sinning could be forgiven through belief in the finished work of Jesus on the cross. This belief could substitute His righteousness for mankind's sin in the sight of the Committee as it had been to Abraham and others that believed in the Committee before and after the cross. Believing in Jesus as the sacrificial Lamb was considered appropriate belief by the Committee after the cross. Believing in the Communicator was also appropriate belief before the cross.

***The mystery revealed now indicated the move by the Committee following the rejection by the Israelite rulers. This period was and is Phase II!! As always mankind is facing the great decision provided by the Committee letting free will determine the destiny of individuals as well as the destiny of nations.*** The seventieth week of Daniel's prophecy was still lacking. The Committee had instituted the hidden gap between the rejection of the Jewish messiah (Jesus) of the Israelites and the seventieth week. This mystery gap had been instituted following the death of Stephen in chapter 7 of the Word. There had been a time following the cross (death, burial, and resurrection of Jesus as the Messiah and Pentecost and Stephen's death) for the Israelites to respond to Jesus being the Messiah as promised. The Israelites continued their rejection to become set aside as recorded in the Word. This mystery period was a gap where the gentiles would have an opportunity to accept Jesus as the sacrificial Lamb. The Israelites were blinded to the recognition of Jesus as the true king and the opportunity to accept Jesus as the true Son was provided to the gentiles (The truth was now divided into two truths. The Jews could believe and accept Jesus as the Lamb or they could also continue in belief following the law and expecting Jesus as king and priest in the future. One truth came from the hidden age of grace and the other truth followed the prophecy given for Israel and their worship system.) The Committee continued to note their plan selecting Paul and planning the mystery age as being successful despite mankind's lack of general recognition and understanding. The change in covenants and placement of Israel was to be considered and compared to the now church (body of Christ and Bride of Christ) age. Paul had been chosen to be the minister to the gentiles in what was to be considered a new age. This new mystery age has also been discussed by mankind as the age of grace. Paul had been converted in a confrontation with the risen Jesus on the road to Damascus. Paul thought and believed he was correct with the intent to continue persecution of the Israelite believers (a remnant). As a result of the confrontation, Paul became a firm believer and carried the true message of Jesus to the gentiles. The message was the death, burial, and resurrection of Jesus with all believers forming one body known as the symbolic body of Christ with Jesus as the Head. Another analogy was Jesus as the bridegroom and the believers as the church becoming participators in the inheritance as adopted sons. The Committee noted that the church now took on a different meaning than in the church as a simple assembly.

***The Special Gap:*** Now entered the unexpected gap period planned by the Committee. As recorded in the Word (This is the correct division between the prophecy since the world began and the Word hidden since the world began . . . between Acts 7 and Acts 8 in the Word.) and after viewing Steven stoned, the witness of Steven served as a final step leading to Paul's determination to do what he thought was the truth. He thought he would do right in destroying a remnant of Israelites at Damascus because of their belief in Jesus being the true Messiah. As per the Word, Paul was met on the road to Damascus by the glorified Jesus as the Christ and underwent a sequence resulting in his conversion and complete dedication to the guidance into the truth. Paul spent some hidden mystery educational time with the Committee and was informed of the completed time of Daniel's seventieth week to be after a time gap where the gentiles would have an opportunity to accept Jesus and the transition through His death, burial, and resurrection. The Committee was pleased again as they noted Paul's about face and his acceptance and carrying of the Word to the gentiles. They set a guideline beyond what Paul was to disclose in his ministry This guideline was simply as it had been with Jesus and with all prophecy given earlier. Certain clues could be given but the true meaning was not fully disclosed about some events to be experienced as time passed. Paul often referred to this as being a thorn in the flesh for him. The thorn was simply that he knew more than he was allowed by the Committee to reveal to

Mankind. (The Committee noted that this was much like mankind as a parent knew more than what was told to a child sometimes.) Paul spent the rest of his life preaching the new dispensation of grace as described in the Word. Paul used the word dispensation to describe the items of the new experience as he preached and taught.

> I Corinthians 9:17 kjv 17 For if I do this thing willingly, I have a reward: but if against my will, a dispensation of the gospel is committed unto me.

> Ephesians 1:10 kjv 10 That in the dispensation of the fulness of times he might gather together in one all things in Christ, both which are in heaven, and which are on earth; even in him:

> Ephesians 3:2 kjv 2 If ye have heard of the dispensation of the grace of God which is given me to you-ward:

> Colossians 1:25 kjv 25 Whereof I am made a minister, according to the dispensation of God which is given to me for you, to fulfil the word of God;

Paul summarized the assignment given to him in the Word as noted by the Committee in Ephesians chapter 3. The Committee noted the discussion to be with the Gentiles and not to the Israelites as a division of truth had been made. Paul's gospel preached unto the Gentiles was simply that Christ had died for sin according to the Word, that He was buried, and that He rose again the third day according to the Word.

I Corinthians 15:1-4 kjv 1 Moreover, brethren, I declare unto you the gospel which I preached unto you, which also ye have received, and wherein ye stand; 2 By which also ye are saved, if ye keep in memory what I preached unto you, unless ye have believed in vain. 3 For I delivered unto you first that which I also received, how that Christ died for our sins according to the scriptures; 4 And that he was buried, and that he rose again the third day according to the scriptures:

Ephesians 3:1 kjv 1 For this cause I Paul, the prisoner of Jesus Christ for you Gentiles, 2 If ye have heard of the dispensation of the grace of God which is given me to you-ward: 3 How that by revelation he made known unto me the mystery; (as I wrote afore in few words, 4 Whereby, when ye read, ye may understand my knowledge in the mystery of Christ) 5 Which in other ages was not made known unto the sons of men, as it is now revealed unto his holy apostles and prophets by the Spirit; 6 That the Gentiles should be fellowheirs, and of the same body, and partakers of his promise in Christ by the gospel: 7 Whereof I was made a minister, according to the gift of the grace of God given unto me by the effectual working of his power. 8 Unto me, who am less than the least of all saints, is this grace given, that I should preach among the Gentiles the unsearchable riches of Christ; 9 ***And to make all men see what is the fellowship of the mystery, which from the beginning of the world hath been hid in God, who created all things by Jesus***

***Christ:*** ¹⁰To the intent that now unto the principalities and powers in heavenly places might be known by the church the manifold wisdom of God, ¹¹According to the eternal purpose which he purposed in Christ Jesus our Lord: ¹²In whom we have boldness and access with confidence by the faith of him. ¹³Wherefore I desire that ye faint not at my tribulations for you, which is your glory. ¹⁴For this cause I bow my knees unto the Father of our Lord Jesus Christ, ¹⁵Of whom the whole family in heaven and earth is named, ¹⁶That he would grant you, according to the riches of his glory, to be strengthened with might by his Spirit in the inner man; ¹⁷That ***Christ may dwell in your hearts by faith;*** that ye, being rooted and grounded in love, ¹⁸May be able to comprehend with all saints what is the breadth, and length, and depth, and height; ¹⁹And to know the love of Christ, which passeth knowledge, that ye might be filled with all the fulness of God. ²⁰Now unto him that can do exceeding abundantly above all that we ask or think, according to the power that worketh in us, ²¹Unto him be glory in the church by Christ Jesus throughout all ages, world without end. Amen.

## *The Extension of the Mystery Gap:*

As indicated, Paul was the apostle selected to provide the recorded Word to the gentiles (and Jews) during the mystery time of grace. This dispensation of Paul's gospel described the believers as being a part of the "body of

Christ." This body is often simply known by mankind as the current church. Paul's inspired words form most of the Word in the New Testament in writing to the gentiles. The Committee recalled the important continuation of the focus on taking the prophetic Word and fulfillment of Jesus to the Israelites only within the Word up through Matthew, Mark, Luke, John, and the beginning seven chapters of Acts after the fulfillment of Pentecost. The recorded words of Paul form the correct truthful teachings of the new covenant to mankind of the current age. (Paul addressed changes brought about in the direct contact mankind had to the Committee. This contact was now through the circumcision by the Holy Spirit in interpretation of mankind's prayers. The Holy Spirit directly translated the prayers to Jesus who was and is an advocate between mankind and the Father. The entire Godhead as the Committee of three in one agreement is now involved together in the position of individual mankind in relation God.) Appropriate acceptable belief in the finished work of Jesus on the cross continues to be needed for mankind to relate appropriately to the Committee. This relationship is for mankind to attain forgiveness of each individual mankind sins past, present, and future.

The continued rejection by the majority of Israelites with the stoning of Stephen brought in the mystery gap designed and planned by the Committee. The "body of Christ" also became symbolically known as the potential "bride of Jesus."

**<u>The Rapture</u>**: The Committee now focused on two major areas of concern noted by mankind in relation to hope projected into the future. One of these major areas of concern was the coming wrath of the Committee based on Daniel's prophecy of the seventieth week and the other was what had become termed as the rapture. These two events had been recorded in the Word by inspiration by Paul.

> Ephesians 5:6 kjv 6 Let no man deceive you with vain words: for because of these things cometh the *wrath of God upon the children of disobedience*.

> Romans 5:9 kjv 9 Much more then, being now justified by his blood, we shall be *saved from wrath through him.*

> I Thessalonians 5:9 kjv 9 For God hath *not appointed us to wrath, but to obtain salvation by our Lord Jesus Christ,*

> I Thessalonians 1:10 kjv 10 And to wait for his Son from heaven, whom he raised from the dead, even Jesus, which *delivered us from the wrath to come.*

The above recorded Word was followed by a discussion of Jesus' return in the air in contrast to His return in vengeance at a later time. The Committee noted the return of Jesus in the air (termed as the "rapture" by mankind) is to remove the true believers of Christ in redemption of their bodies before the wrath and seventieth week of Daniel. Paul recorded this event as follows.

> Romans 8:23 kjv 23 And not only they, but ourselves also, which have the firstfruits of the Spirit, even we ourselves groan within ourselves, waiting for the adoption, to wit, the redemption of our **body**.

I Thessalonians 4:13-18 kjv 13But I would not have you to be ignorant, brethren, concerning them which are asleep, that ye sorrow not, even as others which have no hope. 14For if we believe that Jesus died and rose again, even so them also which sleep in Jesus will God bring with him. 15For this we say unto you by the word of the Lord, that we which are alive and remain unto the coming of the Lord shall not prevent them which are asleep. 16For the Lord himself shall descend from heaven with a shout, with the voice of the archangel, and with the trump of God: and the dead in Christ shall rise first: 17Then we which are alive and remain shall be _caught up together with them in the clouds, to meet the Lord in the air:_ and so shall we ever be with the Lord. 18Wherefore comfort one another with these words.

The Committee noted the division between the Word indicating above that believers at the time of the rapture would escape the wrath to come. The difference in the two comings of Jesus is indicated in Jesus coming in the air and not to the earth in the rapture and then coming in vengeance and landing on the earth in the time of wrath as indicated by the Word below.

II Thessalonians 1:6-8 kjv 6Seeing it is a righteous thing with God to _recompense tribulation to them that trouble you_; 7And to you who are troubled **_rest with us_**, when the Lord Jesus shall be revealed from heaven with his mighty angels, 8_In flaming fire taking vengeance on them that know not God, and that obey not the gospel of our Lord Jesus Christ:_

## *The Coming Seventieth Week:*

> <sup>Romans 11:25 kjv 1</sup>For I would not, brethren, that ye should be ignorant of this **mystery**, lest ye should be wise in your own conceits; that blindness in part is happened to Israel, until the fulness of the Gentiles be come in.

The Committee now discussed the coming seventieth week including the wrath of vengeance. The Word indicates that the blindness of the Israelites will be removed during the final week of Daniel's prophecy. These seven years of prophecy are currently being set up as another transition period.

## Chapter VI
### *Truth 3 Phase III Transition into Seventieth Week*

Chapter VI: Transition into the Seventieth Week

The prophecy of the seventieth week was discussed by the Committee. As in previous times the Committee used and recorded historical events that had set up coming events. For example, very few mankind recognized the important setting up of the Roman era of dominance. Two important items that resulted because of the Roman dominance was 1) the trip to Bethlehem Ephratah by Joseph and Mary (discussed earlier by the Committee) and 2) the dominance by Rome prevented any wars to interrupt the earthly ministry of Jesus. The Committee also discussed their planning of many events such as Jesse being related to David being related to both Joseph and Mary in order to fulfill two important prophecies (Joseph was related to Jesse and had to go to Bethlehem Ephratah to be taxed to fulfill Micah 5:2 in the Word and Mary was the one that was also related to King David and Jesse of Bethlehem Ephratah so that Jesus would then fulfill the Davidic Covenant.) *(The Committee thought that mankind would be amazed why both Mary and Joseph had to be related to King David in order to fulfill the two prophecies at the same time. However, again, most*

***mankind had not recognized their prophetic planning . . . thus, they were now bringing this prophetic feature out of the shadows.)*** Hence, the Committee decided to discuss the use of history to set up for the coming seventieth week of Daniel. They realized as with previous discussions in their current meeting that too many events had happened so they would not have time to discuss all the occurrences being now set up. They also recognized that the finished blindness of the Israelites would come during the latter part of the seventieth week. Hence, they decided to discuss some of the latter more current events provided so that mankind in the current generation should have studied and now relate to.

**The discovery of the United States:** Mankind had often looked into prophecy to try and find the nation of the United States. The Committee noted that due to the mystery age, direct prophecy of many current events had been kept hidden. As a result, mankind continued to miss the division between prophecy and the mystery age. Now as the transition between the mystery age truth (hidden from the beginning of the world but now in existence) and return to the prophetic age truth (revealed from the beginning of the world) was being completed, some of the hidden as well as the prophetic fulfilments was and is now happening for mankind to understand.

The Committee noted that nations continued to be an important part of fulfillment of prophecy and a major part of their plan. Some nations supported Israel and would be blessed while some nations would not support Israel and not be blessed as the Abrahamic covenant of Israel as a nation would continue to be in effect during the seventieth week after the rapture. (Individual mankind missing the rapture would still be under Paul's administration of the cross and the new covenant expressed by Jeremiah in the Word as they moved into the seventieth week.) The remnant of Israel individuals would come to recognize Paul's truth and finally accept Jesus as their true Messiah during the latter half of the seventieth week. Among the nations that continued to support Israel in the final transition as expected by the Committee is the United States. This support by the United States began with the method the United States was developed through the Committee. As they had used nations during prophecy, so they continued to use nations in support of Israel.

The setup of the United States was a beginning of the transition from the mystery age of Paul to the seventieth week of Daniel. Most of mankind's history was hidden in how the Committee had set up the discovery of America and then the development of the United States. Spain had set up their nation to not support the Jews and tried to force them to worship as the Catholics. The Jews refused and many were put in prison and threatened with death. At this time there was an *Italian Jew named Columbus* that found favor by the king and queen of Spain to represent Spain and travel west on an exploratory trip. He was sponsored by Spain and needed sailors for the trip. His sailors were prisoners and Jews for the most part. (Hidden in this event was the Jewish involvement including that Columbus was a Jew. This Jewish connection was not a part of prophecy as this happening was within the mystery age.)

The Committee then related the United States organization as the thirteen colonies. These colonies were noted by the Committee as being similar to the tribes of Israel. This similarity was one of the hidden mysteries and not told by prophecy. Mankind tended to focus on the twelve tribes of Israel but when Israel divided the land promised in the Abrahamic covenant the Committee ended in their plan with thirteen divisions. These divisions of the promised land were to the two sons of Joseph and the other eleven sons of Jacob. (The tribe of Levi as priests inherited none of the promised land.) Thus, there were thirteen colonies in the original land division of the United States and thirteen divisions of the promised land of Israel. (The Committee noted that many mankind called their planned events as accidents, but the Committee knew better.)

The Committee then discussed the separation of Israel into the north and the south and the final conquering of the two parts. They noted that the United States also had a division into the north and the south. However, a president of the United States named Abraham Lincoln was inspired to note the need to keep the whole country together. (They noted that names had always been an important clue for mankind. One of the hidden clues here was that name Abraham.) He was historically reported to indicate that a nation divided could not stand. Hence, the president was inspired to determine by the end result of Israel's division that the civil war of the United States was needed.

Later the Committee noted that the United States as a country began to stray from the basic foundation of their constitution and belief of the founding fathers. The Committee noted in particular a problem resulting from mankind's free will. Satan was at work in those years. Satan carefully changed mankind's understanding of the division between government and true worship of Jesus according to Paul. The forefathers had continually had their worship interrupted by governments (the government of England in particular) so in the writing of the constitution of the United States the Committee had inspired them to declare the separation of church and state. The ideal situation was to **not have the government interfere with the true religion**. However, true religion was considered by the forefathers to help create good government. The Committee noted that **Satan had influenced mankind to reverse the meaning meant by the original statement and now meant for true religion to not interfere with the government while government could interfere with true religion.**

*<u>(The Committee noted and would discuss some more later in the current meeting that Satan continually misguided mankind in using their free will to make decisions contrary to the intent of the Committee. However, the Committee discussed that the free will of individual mankind was the responsibility of each mankind.)</u>*

Therefore, the Committee begin to try and get attention of mankind about the changes being made that was contradictory to procedures being taught through the Word. Mankind often noted these attempts of the Committee but failed to recognize the events as a result of the Committee's planning. Again, the Committee continued to note their planning to get mankind's attention in recognizing the existence of the unseen realm by the seen events. Many of these events were now a part of the mystery and not a part of prophecy although the Committee was setting up for the prophecy to resume. A mix of the prophetic happenings as well as the mystery happenings was now beginning to occur. Even though mankind in the United States began to stray, the United States as a nation continued to support the Jews (now returning to their land). The calendar year of mankind was 1960 when this straying from the truth began to influence the United States' actions. The Committee noted in particular that this influence was to be discussed later in more detail as related to reactions by Satan to some of the hidden mysteries being revealed during the mystery age gap.

One of the amazing set of events provided by the Committee and noted by some of mankind was the following event.

**Entrance of Israel:** The Committee now noted that some prophetic events began to happen as the transition period began to contain elements of the mystery period and some elements of prophecy in setting the stage for the rapture and later the return of week seventy.

The Committee noted that they had arranged the world circumstances to have the nation of Israel to exist again and Israelites to begin to return to their promised land. The Committee had planned for this move as one to get the attention of mankind if they were attentive to the relation of Israel to the Committee throughout history. Lack of attention to this relationship indicated to the Committee how far mankind was straying from knowledge of the Word. The Committee inspired true preaching by some mankind and some written books explaining the truth in prophetic events as they began to happen again. (The Committee noted that the transition period would continue to contain some prophetic events being fulfilled mixed with some hidden mystery events.)

The nation of Israel being set up was witnessed and the nation was recognized by a president of the United States (Harry Truman). Thus, the United States continued to support Israel and continued to be blessed. However, individuals within the United States continued to stray from the study and understanding of the Word. The return of Israel as a nation to fulfill a portion of prophecy occurred in 1948. As Satan began to recognize the movement toward end time fulfillment of prophecy in the Word, he energized Satanic forces to strongly mislead mankind. These energized forces were allowed to take hold specifically in the 1950s and began to cause change in the United States as a focal point. Mankind individual free will and individual responsibility was being tested. The Committee noted that their restriction on Satan led to a limitation on the testing.

> 1 Corinthians 10:13 kjv 13There hath no **temptation** taken you but such as is common to man: but God is faithful, who will not suffer you to be tempted above that ye are able; but will with the **temptation** also make a way to escape, that ye may be able to bear it.

**The Restoration of Jerusalem:** Once Israel became a nation, other nations either supported Israel as a nation or did not support Israel. From Abraham came a current result that was also hidden but now became evident. The nations that resulted from Abraham's son Ishmael and the nation of Israel resulting from Abraham's son Isaac began to dispute the Jews inheritance of the land as supported by the Word. Thus, a war pursued with the Committee supporting the Jews in Israel in what became known by mankind as a six-day war. The new nation of Israel in mankind's calendar year of 1967 won and owned the city of Jerusalem as prophecy indicated.

Later in calendar year of 2019 another president of the United States (Donald Trump) recognized Jerusalem as the appropriate capital of Israel. These present time events were and are a part of setting up the transition into the seventieth week of Daniel's prophecy and the rapture to end the era of mystery. There is no gap between the ending of the mystery age with the rapture and the beginning of the seventieth week of prophecy. However, the season is known due to the transition movements of recorded history and recordings in the Word.

**Getting Attention of Mankind:** Mankind had now continued to stray from the Word and for the most part become as the Committee noted. The Committee noted that most of mankind were now lacking true knowledge to use free-will with correct responsibility. Most of mankind now did not have what the Committee considered true free will, but had now a change guided by Satan. They now had what the Committee determined to be self will. They continued to be self-oriented rather than oriented toward the teachings of the Word. Many of mankind had now been influenced to orient their free will to tend toward not supporting Israel. The United States along with some other nations is now approaching a need to make a decision (to be blessed or not to be blessed),

The Committee continued to try and get the attention of mankind. Many truly inspired preachers of the true Word noted many of the attempts to get the attention of mankind and influence mankind to recognize the Committee and accept the plan of Jesus. The Committee decided to discuss some of these attempts involved in the transition period.

The Committee briefly outlined the structure of main events through history as they had now discussed. They recalled a major goal was to provide substance and evidence for mankind to have faith in belief of the existence of the Committee in their unseen realm. True faith had now centered on belief of Jesus going to the cross and true belief in His death, burial, and resurrection as presented by Paul in the Word.

This involved history includes the discussed prophetic events, the focus on Israel, the earthly ministry of Jesus extending through the death, burial, and resurrection and the coming of the Comforter as promised by Jesus, the blinding of Israel, and into the mystery time of grace as now being continued. **In particular, the Committee was clear that only a part of the Word had now been discussed during their entire meeting. Many more shadows existed with some being truths presented by**

**inspired true believers of the truths in the Word. The truths are being included in inspired publications.**

1. The Committee now discusses some elements of the timeline from beginning to the present time. They knew this view of different ages was important for mankind to know in seeking a better understanding of unseen ages. The Committee knew that mankind had a saying that when you were in the center of a forest, one could not see the forest for the trees. The Committee knew that mankind needed to stand back and view the overall pattern of the different ages. A timeline that the Committee considered beneficial for their discussion included four divisions. These divisions discussed in sequence were 1) gentiles from the beginning to the origination of the nation of Israel, 2) from the beginning of Israel till the beginning of the mystery age, 3) from the mystery age to the beginning of Daniel's week 70, and 4) week 70. This timeline would look as follows.

|------1. gentiles----|-----2. Jews--------|------3. mystery age-----|----4. wk. 70---|

1. Includes time for creation, fall to sin, Noah and ark, Tower of Babel
2. Includes Abraham covenant, Israel creation., King David, Jonah, main prophetic era focus on Israel, Daniel's 69 wks., new covenant in

Jeremiah, earthly ministry of Jesus, Cross, death, burial, resurrection, Passover, death of Stephen, blinding of Israel to sign of Jonah
3. Includes Paul's ministry on death, burial, resurrection, Age of grace, focus on gentiles, rapture presented, United States, Israel return, Jerusalem as capital, other attention getters, approaching time of unbelief like Noah, all blind to sign of Jonah (flexible length to be discussed)
4. 70th week of Daniel's prophecy, includes antichrist, nations decision, mid-week abomination, wrath of Lion of Juda, remnant of Israel unblinded and saved, antichrist and supporting nations defeated (fixed week of years to be discussed).

The Committee begin to discuss and make notes about items mankind should now begin to notice in the plan. The current phase of the Committee's plan was and is to get all individual mankind's attention. Mankind is also to recognize responsibility of mankind to become more and more aware of the unseen realm of the Committee. Mankind should also understand the Committee's existence along with the attributes the Committee has exhibited in the prophetic and mystery age as recorded in the Word. Two major attributes mankind should note is *mercy and longsuffering* toward mankind. This recognition should then support individual mankind's faith in belief of the death, burial, and resurrection of Jesus supplying substance and evidence of the truth indicated in Hebrews of the Word. The following are some items discussed.

1. **To Daniel recorded in the Word: Thy people (the Israelites) and Sign of Jonah**
   The seventy-week prophecy given to Daniel by the Committee was recorded in the Word to be for "thy" people. This makes the 70-week prophetic events to be strictly for the nation of Israel. Jesus also came only to the Israelites as recorded in the Word. He indicated that the only sign the Israelites would get was the sign of Jonah. This was the three days of fulfillment of prophecy by Jesus being in the tomb with His death, burial, and resurrection. Hidden in this Word was that the seventieth week following the mystery age was to focus on Israel. The Committee noted that they had now set Israel into the promised land as a part of the transition. (The seeing of a prophecy being fulfilled when told ahead of time is the plan of the Committee to support mankind understanding about the Committee. The Israelites in general have failed to accept and respond to the fulfillments.)

2. ***Gentiles and Sign of Noah***
   Although the sign of Jonah was provided as a sign for the Israelites, the sign of Jonah also was a sign for the gentiles because ***after*** the sign of Jonah in the death, burial, and resurrection shadowed by coming out of the fish, the Jew Jonah preached ***to the gentiles at Nineveh.*** This action of Jonah was also a hidden ***shadow of what Paul did***. After the

actual death, burial, and resurrection of Jesus, a Jew named Paul preached to the gentiles. However, a new sign was given by Jesus for the gentiles and the Israelites to consider at the end times. Jesus indicated in the Word that at the end, times would be as in the time of Noah. That would be when a small number of mankind was found to still believe in the Committee as desired.

3. **_Fixed time of 1 week_**.
Once the mystery age ended then the length of the 70th week for Israel and the end of time was prophetically determined to be a fixed length of seven years.

4. **_Flexible time of the mystery age_**
The starting time for the mystery age was set and is recorded in the Word. However, the ending time was not recorded in the Word and is not set. Therefore, the beginning of week 70 has not yet been determined either. In between the two times (the mystery age and the 70th week) is the rapture. (This time of division is not when the fulness of the gentiles happens and at the same time the Israelite blindness status stops. These two events will happen at a later time in the latter half of the 70th week.)

5. **_How to measure the flexible time (a mystery but considered imminent)_**
The Committee now considered the next huge event and preparation for it. This was in the Committee's thoughts to be the rapture. The event would usher out the true believers and would usher

in the 70th week. The ending of the mystery age and the beginning of the seventieth week is the same time. The Committee had ready the needed elements for the beginning of the 70th week. However, they had not permitted a specific ending time for the mystery age so they did not present a specific time when the week 70 would begin. They had left this time of division a secret to be declared only by the Father entity on the Committee. During His earthly ministry and recorded in the Word Jesus had stated that only the Father knew the termination of stopping the mystery age with the rapture.

Matthew 24:36 kjv 36But of that day and hour knoweth no man, no, not the angels of heaven, *but my Father only*.

**More Shadows:** The Committee agreed that the only thing mankind is given to determine how the Father might determine the length of this flexible age of mystery is the possible shadows given in the Word. A major event where a length of time was involved was in consideration of the length of time allotted to the existence for Sodom and Gomorrah. Abraham and the angel (the Communicator) discussed lengthening of the existence time for Sodom and Gomorrah. Their discussion centered on how many righteous mankind could be found at that time. Thus, the number of righteous mankind determined the action to be done at Sodom and Gomorrah.

(Assuming mankind accepts this earlier shadow as the method the Father continues to use then ***mankind would actually be the determining factor*** in seeing how long longsuffering and mercy lets the mystery age continue. The number of righteous (current believers standing clothed with the righteousness of Jesus through belief) would be the standard needed in contrast to the time of Noah with unrighteousness (unbelief) being considered by the Father. *<u>Thus, the free will belief or unbelief of mankind would actually determine the flexible length of the mystery age and the beginning of the 70<sup>th</sup> week</u>*. This would also determine when the Father would declare time for the rapture to occur. This method for decision by the Father is also **<u>supported by Jesus' comment about the sign of Noah</u>** being a determining factor. The sign of Noah would be the number of unrighteous or the same would be counting the number of righteous.) The number of unrighteous would be greater than the number of righteous but the total would be all mankind.

The Committee now decided to discuss the current situation for mankind and the use of individual free will decisions to determine the end of the mystery age. The free will decisions are important in the set up for the transition from the mystery age into the 70<sup>th</sup> week.

The length of the flexible period of the mystery age would be determined by the individual mankind free will decisions. The Committee noted that the number of individual free will decisions that were truthful would determine the government of most nations to support Israel and be blessed or to not support Israel and be cursed. They once again discussed the importance that their Word was true as always.

The Committee continued to consider the extended influence of Satan *after he had seen the prophetic fulfillment for the Israelites in 1948 with his influence beginning to take effect in the United States in the 1950s and 1960s*. Satan is greatly energized when recognizing the hidden features of the Committee's plan. Satan was and is energized when faced with the Committee's ability to bring about the prophetic events in revealing the shadows and bringing about the truth of prophecy. He recognized the plan of the Committee and influenced individual mankind's free will decision in misinterpretation of the Word in many churches and in the real-world society. The Committee noted Satan's continued energized influence throughout the time since 1948 in particular as permitted by the Committee but limited as in the shadow found in the Word in Job. They noted that the limits permitted in Job were often considered extreme by mankind.

As a result, mankind had taken actions influenced by Satan that the Committee did not approve. Some of these actions resulted in laws in the nation of the United States that was and is not approved by the Committee. Thus, mankind is now making decisions that is leading to a society approaching the times of Noah. (The Committee noted that the gentiles at Nineveh had changed their ways and prolonged the existence of Nineveh under the message of Jonah before the known shadow of Jonah (to be discussed later). The Committee still decided to try continually to get the attention of mankind in hopes that mankind would meet the ***mystery quota for continued extension of the flexible age of grace.*** The Committee's experience with mankind and foreknowledge through the ages knew that mankind would eventually bring about a society reflecting the age of Noah. This ultimately happened to Nineveh. Mankind's new normal as many mankind termed it had been short lived in the past and would be again even if the Committee could get mankind's attention. Getting mankind's attention often brought about rejection and rebellion as it had in Israel's previous rejection.)

The Committee began to discuss some of the changes made by mankind under the influence of Satan. They remembered and discussed that each individual mankind had the ability to make a free will decision. Thus, they held each individual responsible for the decision each made to believe in the result of the cross or not to believe if they had the ability to understand. Each was responsible for the free will decision made by the individual. The Committee's attribute of mercy continued to be in effect.

Satan knew that the plan of prophecy to help mankind understand about the Committee was to tell historical events ahead of time so when the event happened later in history, mankind would remember and understand the Committee's attribute of foreknowledge. Hence, Satan set out to destroy mankind's knowledge of history. Knowing that the United States had been set up by the Committee to support the Committee's plan for Israel, the United States was one of the prime targets of Satan's plan although not the only one. This influence of Satan had some major effects. The Committee focused on the United States and discussed the following two effects briefly. The Committee noted that they had already briefly commented on these two events but the importance of the influence of Satan in misguiding mankind in making free will decisions was very important in these latter times.

1. The forefathers had created the underlying foundation of the United States to prevent oppression of worship by the government. So, _separation of religion and state was intended to keep state out of interfering with religion._ This was because of the historic interference of Great Britain in colonial time religious worship as well as other things. But Satan influenced mankind to _now reverse the original intent to say no religion in government_. The Committee recognized that their true guidance in the government was needed.
2. A major result of the reversal of saying no religion worship in government was to eliminate teaching of the Committee in educational public schools. This was now contrary to the Word where teaching of worship from generation to generation was expected and a major concern.

There were other major laws passed that were contrary to worship according to the Word. These decisions caused conflicts between true believers and other citizens of the United States. Thus, Satan's influence on mankind's free will decisions continues to lead to conflicts. As a result, mankind's free will with responsibility as presented in the Word had now for some mankind become a self will without responsibility to other mankind (destroying the first and $2^{nd}$ love commandments) as Satan had planned. To some mankind many of the self will decisions seemed rational even though opposed by the Committee. Self will decisions without true responsibility were often now ending in riots resulting in mankind injuring and killing mankind. Many of mankind decisions now have no rational foundational support. Even destruction of law enforcement was and is now happening. (The Committee discussed these events now happening as a result of the lack of true Christian teaching. True Christian related teaching is now being denied in public schools. This was a result of Satan being able to influence some mankind to misinterpret the historical truth as previously discussed. The Committee noted that Satan was continuing to influence mankind to destroy representations of true history such as statues and other signs of the truth. Now because of the misguiding belief of no worship in state supported schools and the breakdown of family units, current generations now had some mankind making decisions in opposition to the Word. Satan's influence on mankind making wrong free will decisions is now having a domino effect.)

The Committee briefly discussed the free will decisions of mankind being influenced by Satan and in direct contrast to the Word. The influence of Satan was now leading mankind to set up the times of Noah as the Committee had seen through foreknowledge. As a result, the Committee had plans as needed for the $70^{th}$ week ready and in place. Unless they could get the attention of mankind and change direction of mankind belief as the Ninevites did when hearing Jonah then the flexible length of the mystery age could be shortened. The choice needed by mankind was simple. Which sign would be considered the most important? Would mankind follow and believe the sign of Jonah created by the Committee or would mankind create the sign of Noah in society.? The Word predicted the sign of Noah to determine the potential extended time of the mystery age as foretold by Jesus.

## Chapter VII

### *Transition Signs of Jonah and Noah*

Many more individual free will decisions by mankind have now been changed through Satan's influence and his success is continuing. The Committee noted that they did not have time to discuss all the changes made by mankind that have been and continue to be led by Satan's influences. As Israel had failed to listen and see the efforts of prophecy and Jesus to help them understand, so many mankind of the world including the United States are in general doing likewise. However, the Committee decided to present some more shadows of prophecy and some mystery events that should get the attention of mankind. The Committee considered these attention getters to focus mankind's attention back on the Word. Although the United States and Israel continue to be focal nations, many of the attention getting actions focused across all mankind. (The Committee noted their interest in each individual mankind.)

**An Important Historical Event:** *The United States as a nation (due to individual free-will voting decisions) will make a major determination for support of the Word in 2020. The nation will support Israel or will decide to* *enter a time of the curse announced by the Word in the Abrahamic covenant.*

***A Convergence:*** One of the attention getters to lead mankind to turn to the Committee for help is a convergence of natural catastrophes, pestilences, mankind errors, etc. The Committee noted that the original earth (like individual mankind) is getting older and approaching a time of being renewed according to their plan. Natural catastrophes, pestilences, and mankind destructions are now causing a convergence of events that should also get mankind's attention. Some of these mentioned by the Committee that mankind has already experienced and will continue to experience are earthquakes, various storms, fires, pestilences, etc. The Committee noted that mankind is their own enemy. The Committee discussed a cartoon of long ago where Pogo the O'possum stated, "I have met the enemy and it R us." For example, the Committee considered the following case. In planning for war, mankind planned to use germ warfare sometimes. Recently experienced is a global epidemic showing what could happen. Mankind's attention was achieved by mankind's error caused by Satan's limited activities but permitted by the Committee. This epidemic should have focused mankind's thoughts back on the plagues of Egypt in Moses' day. Or perhaps on the limitations allowed by Satan in Job's day. Many mankind commented on "a new normal" but the need to pay attention to the Word had competition to be discussed later by the Committee.

***The Four Blood-Red Moons:*** A second attention getter discussed by the Committee was the recent noted occurrence of the four blood-red moons. The dates of the occurrence of each blood red moon provided an opportunity for mankind to have attention drawn to that date and its relation to the Committee's plan. Again, truly inspired mankind discussed the connections and wondered about them. The first blood red moon occurred on **_Passover_** April 15, 2014; the second occurred on the **_Feast of Tabernacles_** October 8, 2014; the third occurred on **_Passover_** April 4, 2015; the fourth occurred on the **_Feast of Tabernacles_** September 28, 2015. Although many mankind wondered about these events, most missed what the Committee had hoped mankind would connect. The **_Passover_** was the first feast and when **_Jesus was_ crucified on the cross** while the **_Feast of Tabernacles_** was when **_Jesus was born (the virgin birth)_**. The meanings of the feasts in connection to prophecy was missed by many of mankind. (_The Committee discussed that many mankind missed the true meaning due to lack of knowledge of the Word. Because of this lack of knowledge mankind continues missing the intent of the signs and opportunities to understand._) Signs in the heavens had been used and is found in various places in the Word. The star of Bethlehem is one that mankind should all know.

> Genesis 1:14 kjv 14And God said, Let there be lights in the firmament of the heaven to divide the day from the night; and **let them be for signs, and for seasons, and for days, and years**:

> Joel 2:30-31 kjv 30And I will shew wonders in the heavens and in the earth, blood, and fire, and pillars of smoke. 31 The **_sun shall be turned into darkness,_**

*and the moon into blood*, before the great and terrible day of the LORD come.

<sup>Revelations 6:12 kjv 12</sup>And I beheld when he had opened the sixth seal, and, lo, there was a great earthquake; and the *sun became black as sackcloth of hair, and the moon became as blood:*

**The Use of Names is a third attempt:** The Committee noted that an attention getting attempt had been briefly mentioned before. They now decided to bring it more up to the current date. The Committee discussed some uses of names in the Word.

One more hidden shadow was discussed and was now being revealed to mankind. It involved the names mentioned in the prophecy and meanings. These were recorded in the Word for mankind to understand in dividing the Word. Among those discussed was the naming of Jacob as Israel so the nation of Israel got a name given by the Committee. Also, the name of Jesus was given by the Committee. Related to the name of the special nation the Word recorded the following as noted by the Committee.

<sup>Genesis 35:10 kjv 10</sup>And God said unto him, Thy **name** is Jacob: thy **name** shall not be called any more Jacob, but Israel shall be thy **name**: and he called his **name** Israel.

<sup>Genesis 35:15 kjv 15</sup>And Jacob called the **name** of the place where God spake with him, Bethel.

The Committee also mentioned another special name. They recognized the name of the perfect sacrifice as a name that all would come to know. His mankind name was also provided by the Committee

> Matthew 1:21 kjv 21 And she shall bring forth a son, and thou shalt call his **name** JESUS: for he shall save his people from their sins.

> Matthew 1:23 kjv 23 Behold, a virgin shall be with child, and shall bring forth a son, and they shall call his **name** Emmanuel, which being interpreted is, God with us.

> Matthew 1:25 kjv 25 And knew her not till she had brought forth her firstborn son: and he called his **name** JESUS.

> Matthew 12:21 kjv 21 And in his **name** shall the Gentiles trust.

At other places in the Word the Committee had set up special names with meaning. The messiah of the prophetic age identified Himself by a name that would continue to be true.

> Exodus 3:14-15 kjv 14 And God said unto Moses, I AM THAT I AM: and he said, Thus shalt thou say unto the children of Israel, I AM hath sent me unto you. 15 And God said moreover unto Moses, Thus shalt thou say unto the children of Israel, the LORD God of your fathers, the God of Abraham, the God of Isaac, and the God of Jacob,

218

hath sent me unto you: this is my name for ever, and this is my memorial unto all generations.

Previously, the mention of using two presidents (Abraham Lincoln and John Kennedy) of the United States in connection to attempt to get the attention of mankind. Now a more direct connection was discussed. Briefly, the names of Abraham in the Abrahamic Covenant are considered connected to Abraham as a president. Also, John is to be connected to John the Baptist or to John the apostle. These connections could only be made if mankind were reminded of the Word. These are shadows that mankind might either wonder about or they would dismiss them as accidents. *The Committee wondered how many such accidents would be needed to get mankind to recognize there has been and are too many accidents!!*

Now a more current attempt to use names of presidents of the United States to show the relationship of the United States to Israel was discussed. (The Committee noted the relationship between these two nations should have a great future unless mankind's free will did as in Israel's past failure.) The Committee noted their continued use of names and relations to make connections to the current time. Two major current connections have occurred using presidents of the United States.

1. President Truman of the United States first gave recognition to the new nation of Israel in 1948

2. President Trump of the United States first gave recognition to Jerusalem being the capital of Israel in 2019.

The return of Israel as a nation in 1948 and the return of Jerusalem being under the control of the Israelites alone were great fulfillments of prophesy as already discussed by the Committee. (Many of mankind had missed this significant set of events, but Satan had not missed the movement by the Committee's plan and has since increased his influence that seemed rational to many mankind. The Committee noted this influence that was limited as in the days of Job in the Word.)

Now the Committee noted the connection of the United States in support of Israel. (The Committee again commented on the Abrahamic covenant statement that supporting Israel would lead to continued blessing of the United States. Now as far as names are concerned, the name Truman can be recognized as True-man and the name Trump can be recognized as short for trumpet. The Committee commented that most mankind would describe these words as just accidents . . .The Committee noted that the following two verses in the Word dealt with the division between the mystery age and the seventieth week. The two verses deal with the rapture.

> I Thessalonians 4:16 kjv 16 For the Lord himself shall descend from heaven with a shout, with the voice of the archangel, and with the **trump** of God: and the dead in Christ shall rise first:

> I Corinthians 15:52 kjv 52 In a moment, in the twinkling of an eye, at the last **trump**: for the **trump**et shall sound, and

the dead shall be raised incorruptible, and we shall be changed.

**_Tower of Babel Connection:_** The Committee continued to discuss the Tower of Babel connection as actually a major shadow for end times. The Committee noted that the time of the Tower of Babel ushered in an age of self will as mankind used free will decisions to think to make themselves equal to their creator. The tower was a shadow that now gained extreme importance in the transition climate leading toward the change from the age of mystery to week 70. The Tower of Babel resulted when mankind got together to build a tower to the heavens. Mankind was then putting themselves equal to the Committee. Mankind was thinking of the creature being equal or even greater than the creator. They focused on making a name for self rather than focusing on the Committee and the Word.

> <sub>Genesis 11:4 kjv 4</sub>And they said, Go to, let us build us a city and a tower, whose top may reach unto heaven; and let **us make us a name**, lest we be scattered abroad upon the face of the whole earth.

The Committee had separated mankind at that time by generating different languages so mankind could not communicate. Hence, work stopped as recorded in the Word. (The Tower of Babel resulted as _mankind developed self-will to lead their free will decisions_ to build the original Tower of Babel.)

**_The End Time Tower of Babel_**: The Committee discussed mankind now creating the foundation for a tower of Babel in the present time and then a future tower of Babel with the antichrist as the leader. This was a major consideration to be after the rapture and to be a major feature of the seventieth week. However, in the current transition period the set up for this future time was already being framed.

The Committee noted that currently a major hidden shadow of nations is the movement of nations to create an end time simulation of the Tower of Babel. The foundation now being formed is the creation of several nations banding together as people did in the days of the original tower. Mankind through interpreters has now become able to communicate so mankind has a method to overcome the separation by language at the original Tower of Babel. The Committee noted two creations of mankind with an opportunity to approach the days of the original Tower of Babel. These two creations now include the European Union and the United Nations. The Committee noted this tower of the end times is to be ruled by the antichrist and provide the launch pad for his end time movements. The Committee noted that this shadow of the Tower of Babel had been hidden from mankind till the present age. The new terms discussed by mankind was and is a global government along with a global church.

Mankind seemingly has not focused on and discussed a replica of the Tower of Babel. The Committee recalled that the Tower of Babel resulted in mankind beginning to think of themselves as equivalent to the creator. The Committee noted that many mankind of today was considering a move toward a global government combined with a global church. This would be like the previous Tower of Babel with mankind creating a similar image of today. The Committee discussed this movement as already a movement to become the development of the future. *More shadows of the global church and the global government was mentioned by the Committee but was left to a later detailed discussion. They decided to discuss the foundation now only in the transition period. They noted that the events in the transition period were becoming difficult to note where the division was between the events in the transition period and the events being in the seventieth week.*

The Committee noted that the movement to globalization of nations banding together and the movement of globalization of churches was and is already sounding good to many of mankind. A few nations and a few churches were destined to not follow this trend. The nations and the churches that followed this trend would be among the ones that would begin to rely on a **_selfish free will_** and think themselves to be able to work together and save themselves when facing any opponent or condition. This attitude would put themselves first and conflict with the first commandment as expressed in the Word. As hidden in the shadows of Daniel's prophecy a few nations to be blessed would remain national and still be supporting Israel. (*Many in the United States opposed President Trump's comments and support for a national view in opposition to the Tower of Babel possibility*.) The nations banding with the antichrist are to be cursed in the future. The Committee noted the continued power in the truth of the Word for the end times following the end of the mystery age and into the seventieth week. The

Committee briefly discussed the continued conflict within the United States to remain national in thinking and also Great Britain in it leaving the European Union. The Committee noted that all these current conflicts in mankind debates seemed to be a result of Satan's influence on the free will of individual mankind. These results continue to set the stage of mankind to either follow the will of the Committee or to follow the will of Satan. Free will of mankind continues to be the responsibility of each individual with the ability to understand. Note that ignorance (lack of understanding) was once a good excuse but not since the cross.

> Acts 17:30 kjv 30And the times of this **ignorance** God winked at; but now commandeth all men every where to repent:

**Mind vs. Heart:** The Committee noted a major problem that was developing with mankind's making of decisions using individual free will. They noted that the problem was the same as mankind deciding to erect a Tower of Babel. Mankind had come a long way in developing technology and were now reaching a state of mind in thinking they had an ability to do anything they needed to solve problems. So, in circumstances of catastrophe and getting through the circumstances some of mankind claimed that God did not do it but mankind through science had done it. Some mankind recognized from the Word that Satan was using his limited powers. The Committee could determine the limitations allowed and determine the curse of a given catastrophe. Some mankind had come to recognize the longsuffering characteristic of the Committee. Many mankind knew that The Committee being One in agreement had the ability to bless or curse in real world circumstances as in the Word. (The Committee could not change their word in the Word, but they could adapt the approach to accomplish the Word but not to conflict with the Word.)

The Committee noted that mankind was now approaching what mankind considered advanced scientific accomplishments. The Committee recognized the scientific abilities of mankind to be a result of being created in the image of the Communicator. This creation placed mankind in a realm of abilities to rule over the other components of the creation presented in the Word. This ability along with an individual reality for each mankind led to the use of free will without responsibility. The lack of responsibility had become a cry by many mankind for freedoms without the needed responsibility to others . . . a selfish attitude now continued to develop in many mankind.

The Committee recognized that the Committee had desired to create an image (mankind) that had instilled in the creation thinking abilities and heartfelt abilities reflecting these abilities of the Committee. The Committee through foreknowledge knew that mankind would also then have this same innate desire as the Committee had. The Committee had planned that mankind would also continue to have similar desires in the future as the Committee had in the creation. Therefore, mankind would (when the time came) want to develop an image in mankind's own likeness. Mankind had now begun to develop what they termed as "smart" devices. Ultimately mankind desired to make these "smart" devices more and more in the image of mankind where the devices could think and even feel as mankind could. So, mankind was now trying to create an image in their own likeness as the Committee had done in the creation.

As a result, mankind is now recognizing a social difference in relation of communication with a technical device. This difference was communication between mankind face to face and communication not face to face using a "smart" device. The Committee knew that this difference would cause a conflict in mankind and that a balance between the two communication features was needed. A basic need for mankind was an innate fellowship component that the Committee had placed into the created being in the original image. Since the Committee desired fellowship with mankind, so mankind desired a similar fellowship. The "smart" devices mankind now had the ability to create lacked this feature of fellowship. Mankind needed to recognize this need . . . and some of mankind had reached this recognition. The created image mankind lacked the abilities of creation of the Committee although as an image they sought these abilities. (The Committee realized that the new resurrected body of Jesus approached many of these desires in an amazing mystery of the future reserved for truthful believing mankind in the rapture.)

The Committee noted that communication had been the problem earlier in the original Tower of Babel along with the basic intent of mankind. So, the basic intent now was beginning to be at fault. It was becoming the same as in the Tower of Babel by placing mankind thoughts on self rather than based on the two basic commandments of the Word. In the Word, this division had been noted as circumcision of the flesh (in the first covenant) and circumcision of the heart (in the second covenant). The latter circumcision was the chosen one in the Word. Mankind needed to note this difference and then actually look at their own situation of decision.

Thus, a situation is now developing that mankind is focusing on the abilities of the mind over faith in the Committee. This is in opposition to belief in the Committee's ability as shown in perfect fulfillment of the Committee's established plan through prophecy. The Committee has always been correct in telling ahead of time historical events that then happened far in the future. They have also hidden in shadows certain truths that have then proven true in reality. All mankind needs to do to understand the truth of the ability of the creators (the Committee) above the creation (mankind) is to review the Word. (The committee noted that mankind could not activate foreknowledge to be perfect in prophetic statements about future events in history while the Committee could.)

This major division between depending on mankind's mind through science and depending on faith to believe in the Committee is a division that the Committee is concerned about. They discussed that many individual mankind making free will decisions could miss their heavenly reward by about eighteen inches between belief in their mind ability and belief in the Committee. The eighteen inches discussed is the approximate distance between the mind and the heart. This is also the difference considered between understanding the circumcision of flesh and the circumcision of the heart. Understanding the circumcision of the flesh is understanding of the shadow of the curtain of the tabernacle destroyed at the cross.

A positive comment by mankind was the development of a new normal. The Committee noted that the new normal could be to return to a study of the Word and to the truth. Again, this decision was one of individual actions of free will. The Committee noted that in the United States, a section of the Individuals was using hate to determine their free will decisions. They hoped that a majority of individual mankind would use the abilities resulting from being created in the image of the Committee for constructive free will decision making. Once again, the Committee determined that free will decision making without responsibility would help create a society as in Noah's time and decrease the length of the flexible mystery age.

------gentiles----|-----Jews--------|------mystery age-----|----wk. 70---|

The resulting timeline A or B structured below is dependent on the free will decision of mankind. The difference is the length of the mystery age. In timeline A the mystery age is extended as mankind heeds the sign of Jonah. In timeline B the mystery age is shortened due to mankind neglecting the sign of Jonah and therefore creating the times of Noah. Mankind heeding the sign of Jonah should lengthen the time of belief resulting in the shadow of Nineveh and shown in timeline A.

A. |---gentiles---|---Jews---|==***mystery age***======|---wk. 70---|
B. |---gentiles---|---Jews---|=***mystery age***=|---wk. 70---|

**A Shadow of the Rapture:** The Committee committed briefly on the event to divide the present age of grace (undeserved mercy) and the last seven years (of tribulation). This event is recorded as one of the mysteries found when the truth in the Word is correctly divided and revealed to Paul through inspiration of the Committee. The rapture is one event studied by interested mankind and in particular by Christians of true faith. The Committee recognized the rapture as one of power demonstrated by the shepherd (Jesus the Christ) as He appears in the air to draw His sheep (true to the Word) to Him (as a shadow of physical lightning). The Committee knew that Jesus had indicated He was and is the light of the world in the Word. The Committee noted that this analogy is a remaining mystery that mankind has come to in mankind's study of science. Mankind has now come to the realization that light is where matter is changed into energy or vice versa. Hence, this is a view of the rapture where a change in the physical body is a mystery reflected by Jesus in His resurrection as the first fruit. He could then pass through physical walls and still do physical activities according to His appearances after the resurrection. He demonstrated His power at this time in the Word.

A major shadow of the resurrection has been provided for mankind to view. God (the Committee) has allowed mankind a mind of science to develop many new things. (The present time is one of tremendous exploration and discovery as predicted in the Word. Remember that mankind and descendants has inherited the being created in the image of the Committee. Hence, mankind is above all other living creations in abilities of the mind.) Mankind of science have now discovered what has been defined as the electromagnetic pulse harnessing a very powerful source. This electromagnetic pulse can be turned off and on with the pressing of a button. It is instantaneous and is used for example in lifting cars in a junk yard as well as in other areas of use. This source of power controlled by mankind is a great shadow of the rapture. As an electromagnet can raise a car when turned on, in a mysterious similarity Jesus can attract true Christians into the air for the rapture.

According to the Word, true faith is a substance. Faith as a substance is an attraction between the Shepherd and His sheep. When the true shepherd (Jesus the Christ) appears in the air, a **similar event to the shadow** shown to mankind in the real-world electromagnetic pulse will happen. **(What created mankind can create, the Creators of mankind can create much greater.)** The sheep will undergo a transformation that will be due to the physical shadow of lightning and the powerful attraction of faith will enable the shepherd to fulfill the rapture as recorded in the Word. The Committee noted that the Word continues to be true and fulfill prophecy as presented from the foundations including the mysteries kept hidden from the foundation of the world. All of the prophecies and mysteries are currently being revealed through mankind's history and shown **Out of the Shadows.**

**Mankind. Free Will, and Two Signs:** As the Committee begin to consider adjournment, they summarized some important truths for mankind in the present mystery age. As they approached adjourning, they knew there was a special shadow of an imminent appearance of the Bridegroom and a kingdom to come. All true believers would be invited. This event is still in the near future at the end of the flexible time of the mystery age as discussed by the Committee.

All mankind (Jew and Gentile) now have two major signs to consider for the future. Each individual using individual free will is responsible (even though many ignore the responsible part) to make an important decision about the signs.

The individual mankind that understood the sign of Jonah and accepted in true belief what Jesus did in substitution of His righteousness for the individual mankind's sins then that individual mankind would be counted in the possibility to extend the flexible length of the mystery age. This would provide more time for other mankind to become believers.

The individual mankind that failed to understand the sign of Jonah would automatically fall into being counted in society as falling in the major sign of Noah's time. These individual's would be counted as not following the sign of Jonah as needed to be saved in the rapture represented in the shadow of the harvest by Jesus in His earthly ministry and expressed in the written Word by the living Word (The gospel of John, Ch. 1).

As the division of the truth has been important from the beginning, mankind has been held responsible by the Committee to respond to their plan. The Committee's plan for mankind to understand the unseen realm of the Committee has now been almost all revealed through the ages. The Committee knew the plan had provided early prophecy and continued to show later prophecy to help support understanding by mankind. Even now many revelations are continuing to be shown from **_out of the shadows_**. Speaking about the shadows created by the light, the Committee noted that as the light shines, shadows are developed and revealed. Mankind could stay in the shadows of dark understanding or move out of the shadows with understanding in light. Reality came out of the shadows as understanding of the unseen realm by the seen realm as intended by the Committee through the developed Word. This understanding by mankind has been the Committee's plan from the beginning of time for mankind. Now mankind should be understanding the framework of the plan.

**Mankind's Late Great Opportunity:** As the Committee continued to approach adjournment, they noted that mankind currently faces a similar real-world situation that Israel faced and failed. The Committee discussed another _historical hidden shadow that has now been shown twice_. When the nation of Israel left Egypt and was led to the border of the promised land according to the Abrahamic covenant they were not allowed to enter because of their unbelief in the Committee. Thus, the time was extended for forty years in the wilderness while a generation of unbelief was replaced by a new generation. Then many years later a second opportunity to see and hear and believe in the Committee's plan was given directly to Israel in the ministry of Jesus. The Committee recalled that prophecy had provided Israel substance and evidence to have faith and recognition that Jesus was the **I Am** fulfilling the prophecy provided ahead of time and now including all mankind. However, Israel missed the truth and suffered the consequences a second time as revealed in the Word.

Would the current generation of mankind also miss the truth and suffer consequences, or would they remember the worldwide crises recently revealed as a possibility in the future? The Committee noted that the work of Satan as allowed had caused the recent world crises. The Committee discussed that the current wrath of Satan could not be compared to the coming wrath of the Lion of Judah. This was presented in Paul's guided ministry in an often-hidden message related to who would be responsible for the final delusion given to unbelieving mankind during the final fixed week of Daniel. This belief in the delusion due to ignorance of mankind would bring in the time of the wrath of the Lion of Judah at the end of the seventieth week of fixed length. (The Committee had allowed Satan to create the current plague across the whole world in another major attempt to get the focus of mankind to return to the truth in the Word. An extension of the flexible time of mystery or grace continued to be discussed and desired by the Committee. This extension was desired by the Committee in agreement as One.) The Committee wanted mankind to recognize who would send (allow) the strong delusion on into the seventieth week. Also, this strong delusion is not to be for true believers as true believers (participants in the harvest rapture) will have departed before this wrath of the Lion of Judah. This delusion will make any belief in the Committee very difficult after the main harvest.

> 2 Thessalonians 2:8-12 kjv 8And then shall that Wicked be revealed, whom the Lord shall consume with the spirit of his mouth, and shall destroy with the brightness of his coming: 9Even him, whose coming is after the working of Satan with all power and signs and lying wonders, 10And with all deceivableness of unrighteousness in them that perish; because they received not the love of the truth, that they might be saved. 11And for this cause **God shall send them strong delusion**, that they should believe a lie: 12That they all might be damned *who believed not the truth, but had pleasure in unrighteousness.*

The Committee also discussed that the Word warned all mankind:

> Hebrews 10:31 kjv 31It is a fearful thing to fall into the hands of the living God.

Most of mankind had come to rely on their belief in the mercy of the Committee and had an ignorance of the future justice feature of the Committee to be seen in the coming judgement during the seventieth week. The Word would continue to be truth. Mankind had in general become ignorant of the following Word related to wisdom.

> Psalm 111:10 kjv ¹⁰**The fear of the LORD is the beginning of wisdom:** a good understanding have all they that do his commandments: his praise endureth for ever.

The Committee continued to discuss the Word including this warning and prefacing the warning with a straightforward reminder for mankind. This preface reminds mankind of what they cannot now claim ignorance of through unbelief. Again, the Committee discussed that the Word reminded mankind of the coming wrath of the Lion of Judah during the seventieth week and they discussed their plan providing substance and evidence establishing support of faith in the Committee's unseen existence. Ignorance is not now to provide an excuse or reason for unbelief!! The preface is presented as having been a <u>**shadow but now revealed in the fulfillment of the true image.**</u>

> Hebrews 1:1-31 kjv ¹⁰For the law having a **shadow of good things to come, and not the very image of the things**, can never with those sacrifices which they offered year by year continually make the comers thereunto perfect. ²For then would they not have ceased to be offered? because that the worshippers once purged should have had no more conscience of sins. ³But in those sacrifices there is a remembrance again made of sins every year. ⁴For it is not possible that the blood of bulls and of goats should take away sins. ⁵Wherefore when he

cometh into the world, he saith, Sacrifice and offering thou wouldest not, but **a body hast thou prepared me**: ⁶In burnt offerings and sacrifices for sin thou hast had no pleasure. ⁷Then said I, Lo, I come (in the volume of the book it is written of me,) to do thy will, O God. ⁸Above when he said, Sacrifice and offering and burnt offerings and offering for sin thou wouldest not, neither hadst pleasure therein; which are offered by the law; ⁹Then said he, Lo, I come to do thy will, O God. <u>He taketh away the first, that he may establish the second.</u> ¹⁰By the which will we are sanctified through the offering of the body of Jesus Christ **once for all**. ¹¹And every priest standeth daily ministering and offering oftentimes the same sacrifices, which can never take away sins: ¹²But this man, after he had offered one sacrifice for sins for ever, sat down on the right hand of God; ¹³From henceforth expecting till his enemies be made his footstool. ¹⁴For by one offering he hath perfected for ever them that are sanctified. ¹⁵Whereof the Holy Ghost also is a witness to us: for after that he had said before, ¹⁶<u>This is the covenant</u> that I will make with them after those days, saith the Lord, I will put my laws **<u>into their hearts</u>**, and **<u>in their minds</u>** will I write them; ¹⁷And their sins and iniquities will I remember no more. ¹⁸Now where remission of these is, there is <u>no more offering for sin</u>. ¹⁹Having therefore, brethren, boldness to enter into the holiest by the blood of Jesus, ²⁰By a new and living way, which he hath consecrated for us, **<u>through the veil, that is to say, his flesh;</u>** ²¹And having an high priest over the house of God; ²²Let us draw near with a true heart in full assurance of faith, having our hearts sprinkled from an evil conscience, and our bodies washed with pure water. ²³Let us hold fast the profession of our faith without wavering; (for he is faithful that promised;) ²⁴And let us consider one another to provoke unto love and to good works: ²⁵Not forsaking the assembling of ourselves together, as the manner of some is; but exhorting one another: and so much the more, <u>as ye see the day approaching.</u> ²⁶For if we <u>sin wilfully after that we have received the knowledge of the truth,</u> there remaineth no more sacrifice for sins, ²⁷But a certain fearful looking for of judgment and fiery indignation, which shall devour the adversaries. ²⁸He that despised Moses' law died <u>without mercy</u> under two or three witnesses: ²⁹Of how much sorer punishment, suppose ye, shall he be thought worthy, who hath trodden under foot the Son of God, and **hath counted the blood of the covenant,** wherewith he was sanctified, **an unholy thing**, and hath done despite unto the Spirit of grace? ³⁰*<u>For we know him that hath said, Vengeance belongeth unto me, I will recompense, saith the Lord. And again, The Lord shall judge his people.</u>* ³¹*<u>It is a fearful thing to fall into the hands of the living God.</u>*

The Committee noted the solution as recorded in the word.

2 Chronicles 7:14 kjv ¹⁴If my people, which are called by my name, shall humble themselves, and pray, and

seek my face, and **turn from** their wicked ways; then will I hear **from** heaven, and will forgive their sin, and will heal their land.

The Committee again mentioned that individual mankind in particular within the special nation of the United States (as with mankind in the nation of Israel) now faced a big free will decision in determining the Father's extension of the flexible age of grace and longsuffering.

The Committee noted at least four misguided influences of Satan since he had started to increase his works after the 1948 prophecy fulfillment and following events of prophecy with Israel had started. The influence of Satan began to take effect in the 1950s and since then the following influences provided wrongful increases. First, the Satanic movement has been to take all Word influence out of government. (The Committee discussed a major component of this movement as taking the needed influence of the Word out of public schools.) Satan has misled mankind to misinterpret the intended historical intention to separate government and Christianity by keeping government out of religion as this had continually been a problem to the forefathers of the United States. The forefathers sought to keep this feature from happening in the United States. The misinterpretation by mankind is now to keep religion out of government which has been a major goal of Satan. Second, has been to continue the Satanic influence to push abortions in killing babies to the extent of killing full term babies. (The Committee noted that these were all to be in heaven based on the Committee's law of mercy. The Committee also noted that because of the first and second influences of

Satan on mankind's free will decision making, Satan had been able to under mind the Committee's influence from the Word in providing a good supporting foundation for the youth of mankind.) The third influence was like unto that of Satan in Sodom and Gomorrah that the Committee destroyed in an earlier time. The fourth influence that was now being increased was the destruction of marriage with mankind living together without first marrying. In these along with other movements of mankind that had resulted from the increased influence of Satan the United States was being put into a sad position. Many mankind had now come to recognize the occult as the unseen free will choice under the Satanic delusion. The Committee knew that the flexible time of mystery would eventually end and the fixed time of the seventieth week would happen. The sign of Noah's time would eventually happen in the middle of the fixed week as the sign of Jonah faded.

Now the Committee knew in the current time the nation of the United States has a great opportunity to recognize the certainty of a coming vengeance of the Lion of Judah. His returning to the earth during the seventieth week of fixed length would be in vengeance against Satan and all sin as a majority of mankind will have ignored the free will acceptance of the gift possible through the cross. There was a time that the Committee blinked at this ignorance but no more.

The Committee discussed that ignorance of the fulfillment and opportunity of mankind now had grown across the entire world. The Committee knew they had provided substance and evidence for current mankind across the world to not be able to claim ignorance of what Jesus had accomplished. Even though not being eye-witnesses, history through prophecy as recorded by truthful mankind and in the Word is the witness. (The Committee knew what mankind in general would eventually do. However, currently mankind could in making individual free will decisions of belief extend the mystery age as the city of Nineveh in Jonah's age. (Mankind should now know the truth of the sign of Jonah.) The Word recorded how mankind of Nineveh (gentiles) through belief had their time extended in the times of Jonah (a Jew). Later, as mankind had always done, the majority of mankind in Nineveh returned to be as the majority in the times of Noah. The Committee knew by foreknowledge that even if a remnant of mankind responded to refocus toward a new normal using the truth of the Word through an immediate belief, the majority would continue in nonbelief as in the days of Noah. This trend of mankind toward condoning a society as in the days of Noah had been recorded by Jesus during His earthly ministry. So was and is the Committee's discussion of the truth in the Word.)

Peter through the Word presented the following to Israel when they had denied the truth:

> Acts 3:13-23 kjv 13 The God of Abraham, and of Isaac, and of Jacob, the God of our fathers, hath glorified his Son Jesus; whom ye delivered up, and denied him in the presence of Pilate, when he was determined to let him go. 14 But ye denied the Holy One and the Just, and desired a murderer to be granted unto you; 15 And killed the Prince of life, whom God hath raised from the dead; whereof we are

witnesses. ¹⁶And his name through faith in his name hath made this man strong, whom ye see and know: yea, the faith which is by him hath given him this perfect soundness in the presence of you all. ¹⁷And now, brethren, I wot that **through ignorance** ye did it, as did also your rulers. ¹⁸But those things, which God before had shewed by the mouth of all his prophets, that Christ should suffer, he hath so fulfilled. ¹⁹Repent ye therefore, and be converted, that your sins may be blotted out, when the times of refreshing shall come from the presence of the Lord; ²⁰**And he shall send Jesus Christ**, which before was preached unto you: ²¹Whom the heaven must receive until the times of restitution of all things, which God hath spoken by the mouth of all his holy prophets **since the world began.** ²²For Moses truly said unto the fathers, **A prophet** shall the Lord your God raise up unto you **of your brethren**, like unto me; him shall ye hear in all things whatsoever he shall say unto you. ²³And it shall come to pass, that every soul, which will not hear that prophet, shall be destroyed from among the people

The Committee noted that Jesus was that prophet.

The Committee also pointed out that Paul had continued in his ministry to be guided by them to issue a warning in the Word that ignorance would not be dealt with as under the Law of Moses. The true sacrifice was the Lamb (Jesus) on the cross. No other sacrifice would ever take the truth of the cross away. Paul was guided to present the truth on Mars hill as:

> Acts 17:29-31 kjv 29Forasmuch then as we are the offspring of God, we ought not to think that the Godhead is like unto gold, or silver, or stone, graven by art and man's device. 30**And the times of this ignorance God winked at; but now commandeth all men every where to repent:** 31Because he hath appointed a day, in the which he will judge the world in righteousness by that man whom he hath ordained; whereof he hath given assurance unto all men, in that he hath raised him from the dead.

Paul continued to be guided by the Committee to present to the gentiles the message that the Israelites missed. The Committee noted that Paul had presented the fullness of Christ. He also indicated that some gentiles were continuing is ignorance. Paul also encouraged gentiles that believed to continue in belief and not to listen to the ignorance. The Law had now been placed by circumcision of the heart of believers and ignorance of this new age with the true sacrifice was not a truth to which believers were blind. Ignorance can no longer be an excuse for most. (The Committee acknowledged in their discussion that **mercy** was one of their attributes that took care of mankind who being too young or having an inability to understand lacked knowledge of the true sacrifice. Others were declared guilty of sin and would face the sentence of two deaths!)

> Ephesians 4:17-27 kjv 17This I say therefore, and testify in the Lord, that ye henceforth walk not as other Gentiles walk, in the vanity of their mind, 18Having the understanding darkened, being alienated from the life of God through the **ignorance that is in them,**

**because of the blindness of their heart:** ¹⁹Who being past feeling have given themselves over unto lasciviousness, to work all uncleanness with greediness. ²⁰But ye have not so learned Christ; ²¹If so be that ye have heard him, and have been taught by him, as the truth is in Jesus: ²²That ye **put off** concerning the former conversation **the old man**, which is corrupt according to the deceitful lusts; ²³And be renewed in the spirit of your mind; ²⁴And that ye put on the **new man**, which after God is created in righteousness and true holiness. ²⁵Wherefore putting away lying, speak every man truth with his neighbour: for we are members one of another. ²⁶Be ye angry, and sin not: let not the sun go down upon your wrath: ²⁷Neither give place to the devil.

***Identification of the Committee:*** The Committee decided to identify the three members. The identities were provided in the Word. The three were commonly known by mankind of knowledge as the Father, Son, and Holy Ghost as identified in the Word. The Committee recognized Jesus as the Christ or Word as in the scriptures (John 1, kjv). The Committee was recognized by Peter in the Word as ***the determinate Counsel***. The Committee also recognized the truth in dividing the one creation as identified from the beginning as heaven and earth (one invisible and one visible). The mystery of the three entities in one agreement would remain.

Matthew 28:18-20 kjv ¹⁸And Jesus came and spake unto them, saying, All power is given unto me in ***heaven and***

***in earth.*** ¹⁹Go ye therefore, and teach all nations, baptizing them in the ***name of the Father, and of the Son, and of the Holy Ghost:*** ²⁰Teaching them to observe all things whatsoever I have commanded you: and, lo, I am with you alway, even unto the end of the world. Amen.

Acts 2:22-24 kjv ²²Ye men of Israel, hear these words; Jesus of Nazareth, a man approved of God among you by miracles and wonders and signs, which God did by him in the midst of you, as ye yourselves also know: ²³***Him, being delivered by the determinate counsel and foreknowledge of God***, ye have taken, and by wicked hands have crucified and slain: ²⁴Whom God hath raised up, having loosed the pains of death: because it was not possible that he should be holden of it.

***The Discussion of Time:*** The Committee decided to end their meeting by discussing what to expect in the ending of the flexible length of the mystery time (Also this point in time was noted as the same as the beginning of the seventieth week.). They wanted to make a major point on the attention and focus of mankind on the individual free will decisions to be made as Paul had indicated. The Committee discussed their desire for mankind to make a decision to recognize the sign of Jonah and the Committee's existence in the unseen realm. The Committee noted then as in the days of Noah, a minority of mankind would have true belief exhibited by following the Committee's plan. Also discussed in the Word, a majority of mankind had again been misled by Satan and

Satanic forces into misinterpretation in the length of the age of mystery. Mankind in misinterpretation of the already extended flexible length of time (since the Committee has now already extended the length of the age of mystery) has many that declared "God was dead!" showing the influence of Satan again. However, the Word through Peter included a truthful report of the longsuffering of the Committee. The Committee noted the connection by the Word of longsuffering in the time of Noah with the continued longsuffering in the present time of mystery. They were reminded of Jesus' comment of the end times being as the times of Noah.

> 1 Peter 3:20 kjv 20 Which sometime were disobedient, <u>when once the **longsuffering** of God waited in the days of Noah, while the ark was a preparing</u>, wherein few, that is, eight souls were saved by water.
> 2 Peter 3:9 kjv 9 The Lord is <u>not slack concerning his promise, as some men count slackness; but is **longsuffering** to us-ward, not willing that any should perish, but that all should come to repentance.</u>
> 2 Peter 3:15 kjv 15 And <u>account that the **longsuffering** of our Lord is salvation</u>; even as our beloved brother Paul also according to the wisdom given unto him hath written unto you;

**Two Time Periods in Focus:** The Committee now continued to discuss the two major time periods in more detail. The Committee desired for mankind to focus and understand these two remaining time periods and the determining factor resulting in the length of time left. *One was a flexible indeterminate time period and one was a set time.* The prophetic finish of time included a final seventieth week of years as presented through Daniel and set in length of time by the Committee. The seventieth week of years would be a fixed seven years in length. The mystery time period was not fixed in length of time but flexible and *not determined by the Committee.* (Mankind was to be reminded that the individual free will was a determining factor of mankind that the Committee had fixed in the creation. The Committee wanted the created image to decide to relate to the Committee out of love denoted by the first of the two commandments presented by Jesus. The Committee did not want to force mankind to obey but the Committee noted true love and obedience to be out of mankind's free will. The Committee desired love returned freely with a returned service of love rather than by force.)

> Mark 12:28-31 kjv 28 And one of the scribes came, and having heard them reasoning together, and perceiving that he had answered them well, asked him, Which is the first commandment of all? 29 And Jesus answered him, The first of all the commandments is, Hear, O Israel; The Lord our God is one Lord: 30 And thou shalt love the Lord thy God with all thy heart, and with all thy soul, and with all thy mind, and with all thy strength: this is the first commandment. 31 And the second is like, namely this, Thou shalt love thy neighbour as thyself. There is none other commandment greater than these.

The discussion of the two time periods continued. The time of the end of the mystery was at a time not prophesied when the rapture would occur. The end of the set time (the seventieth week) would culminate in the second coming of Jesus to the earth as the **_Lion of Judah_** as indicated in the avenge foretold in the Word of Revelations through the apostle John. The end of the flexible time (the mystery age) would be another coming of Jesus in the air **_as the Lamb_** and recorded in the ministry of Paul. This coming in the air was to gather a harvest of believers and often discussed by the believers in teachings by Paul (known by mankind as the rapture).

**_What was to determine the ending of the flexible period?_** The standard needed had continually been indicated in shadows and even direct results presented in the Word. Perhaps one of the most famous indications on the flexible of endings was in times past and was recorded in the Word. Although already briefly mentioned, the importance of this in the plan was again discussed. The discussion between Abraham (Abram) and the messenger representing the Committee created a shadow for the present time leading up to the present society of Jesus' sign of Noah. The length of time for Sodom and Gomorrah depended on mankind and their free will decision to believe and serve the Committee as intended. The Committee noted that numbers of believers in the Committee and their glorification of the Committee through belief was important. The Committee focused on at least a remnant of believers to result as determined by mankind. However, the number that made an appropriate decision to be clothed in the righteousness of Jesus provided through true belief in the substitution provided on the cross continued to be of utmost importance to the Committee. (Several times in the Word the Committee had in past times decided to either extend time periods or not . . . especially in destinies of nations, in lives of men, . . . but even in the time of Noah!!)

Now the Committee discussed and noted that mankind had no choice in the length of the seven years remaining according to Daniel's prophecy ending in the Lion of Judah returning. However, the Committee discussed the flexible time for the ending of the mystery time period of Paul. This ending was flexible but decided by the Father member of the Committee. The decision for when Jesus would return in what was known by inspired and true interpretation by mankind as the rapture following the shadow of the destruction of Sodom and Gomorrah and of the destruction at the time of Noah seemed to indicate the number of righteous mankind (which also indicated the number of unrighteous). Thus, the shadows indicate the end of the flexible period of grace should be determined by the free will glorification service of mankind believers. Mankind should now be aware of this expected unknown standard of the Father member and mankind's ability to extend the flexible end of the mystery age. This revelation should come from expectation found in the Word. Putting together the numbers of righteousness needed in the days of Sodom and Gomorrah and the lack of righteousness numbers as the sign of Noah is meant to lead mankind to this standard of expectation by the Father. <u>Mankind should recognize that the number of righteous is actually the same as counting the number of</u>

*unrighteous often considered in discussing the times of Noah.* As the number of righteous decreases then the number of unrighteous increases as in the times of Noah. Thus, counting the righteous in Sodom and Gomorrah was the same as counting the unrighteous.

The Committee noted that they would continue to get some of mankind to recognize and focus on the determination of the end of the flexible mystery age. Of major importance was that a majority of mankind in the world had recently noted that they did need to refocus following the recent global attention attempt letting Satan use the pandemic plague. Manny mankind had named this choice as choosing a new normal. A major problem noted by the Committee was that mankind was beginning to think mankind could overcome and be the winners due to their own brain power and ingenuity. This was leading to a major conflict with the Word. The Committee decided to discuss the problem a little later at another meeting.

The Committee now looked at mankind's free will choice in ending the mystery age of Paul and entering the final week of Daniel's prophecy with the set time ending in seven years. The end timeline now presented two possibilities. One was considered by the Committee as indicated with a longer mystery period based on a continued extension with mankind setting a foundation of belief in the sign of Jonah (now understood to represent Jesus and the preaching of a Jew (Paul) to gentiles). The other timeline would have a shorter mystery period based on a lack of mankind's free will following a belief in the sign of Jonah and determining a fast development of society reflecting a time of Noah.

**_The Hidden Shadow of the Harvest:_** The Committee discussed another shadow hidden in the Word. The harvest was used in the Word by Jesus in a variety of ways. The parable of the seed was one way. The difference between the wheat and the tares was another presentation by Jesus. However, a major shadow was hidden in the Word and found in the truth of the revelation hidden among other hidden shadows in the history of Boaz and Ruth. The Committee briefly summarized the harvest of Barley as they had developed it. The three phases of the Barley harvest were hidden as shadows of how the harvest of the true believers would unfold. These true believers were ones that had received the seal of the Holy Spirit in attaining the substitution of the righteousness of Jesus as the Christ in exchange for a sinful status. The three phases now being revealed by some inspired mankind follow.

**_The Barley Harvest Shadow:_** The barley harvest consisted in three parts. The first part came when the grain first began to develop. This picking of the barley at this early age was known as the first fruits and was selected from among the first productive barley in the field.

A second collection of the harvest was the time when the barley field was ready with the grain fully developed. Then the harvest was the largest amount of good production.

As the second phase of harvest was accomplished, some of the gleanings were left in the field. These gleanings were then harvested at a later time.

Leviticus 19:9-10 kjv ⁹And when ye reap the harvest of your land, thou shalt not wholly reap the corners of thy field, neither shalt thou gather the gleanings of thy harvest. ¹⁰And thou shalt not glean thy vineyard, neither shalt thou gather every grape of thy vineyard; thou shalt leave them for the poor and stranger: I am the LORD your God.

The Committee noted that many hidden shadows in the Word could not be fully discussed in this particular meeting. They did discuss briefly that the Word in Ruth found a revelation of Israel represented by Naomi and a gentile named Ruth along with an Israelite kinsman named Boaz. Hidden in the history recorded in the Word was a representation of the relation between the Israelites, the gentiles, and a kinsman shadowing Jesus as a kinsman. Mankind should begin to recognize this shadow.

Back to the shadow of the harvest as it really became evident through the Word in the hidden revelation in Ruth and in the teachings of the harvest by Jesus in His ministry.

To make a shorter version, Jesus was the first fruit and the saints resurrected right behind Jesus at the time of His death, burial, and resurrection were represented as the first fruits before the larger harvest. The Committee recognized a latter large harvest to be when the rapture would occur.

The gleanings would be a smaller number of believers to be gathered during the seventieth week. The gleanings would also be babies born under the mercy of the Committee. (The previous shadow was the forty-year journey of the Israelites to the promised land when only two of the original generation entered after the forty years.) Also, included in the three phases would be all mankind that were born again as indicated by the shadow of the second birth to Nicodemus in the Word.

> John 3:3-5 kjv ³Jesus answered and said unto him, Verily, verily, I say unto thee, Except a man be born again, he cannot see the kingdom of God. ⁴Nicodemus saith unto him, How can a man be born when he is old? can he enter the second time into his mother's womb, and be born? ⁵Jesus answered, Verily, verily, I say unto thee, Except a man be born of water and of the Spirit, he cannot enter into the kingdom of God.

**_Emphasis back to the two ages:_** Now the Committee returned to focus their discussion on the two ages where one age was to end, and the other age was to begin. The Committee's attention on these major components of the transition was continued. Currently the reason for extending this discussion of the two ages was that based on the shadows mankind was to determine this boundary between the two times. The Committee discussed that the present time being flexible was an important concept for mankind to understand. The Committee remembered that the age of mystery was not fixed, and the continued mystery was that the Committee had relinquished control over the length of this period. They had kept control of the length of the seventieth week. ***Thus, they actually retained no control over when the division between the age of mystery ended and the final seven weeks of time***

***would begin***. (Inspired mankind has in the present time indicated that there seems to be no prophetic signs prior to Jesus to watch for the rapture. These two signs as one is determined by mankind. The Committee mentioned that the time of Noah was before the Israelite nation existed so it would apply to the gentile age.) Now the Committee began to discuss two major opposing forces in determining the length of the flexible length of the mystery age. One force would extend the flexible period and one force would shorten the flexible period unless mankind could appropriately handle both forces as the Committee had done.

**What was to determine the ending of the flexible period?** Two major opponents were noted by the Committee in conflict to bring about the end of the flexible period. As in the Tower of Babble, the two opponents would be from free will decisions of mankind. The free will decisions would either follow decisions based on the true Word or the decisions would be based on self-reliance on the intelligence of mankind. These two opposing decision processes were discussed by the Committee as focusing on two major components in creation of mankind. One component was focusing on the heartfelt relationships of mankind and the second component was focusing on the intellect and ability to adapt to environmental changes. The two components were to work together as directed in the early Word at creation. However, mankind was supposed to recognize the appropriate working of the two abilities together. In contrast, Satan had influenced mankind to focus on self-reliance on mankind's own intelligence and ability to conquer any problem without reference to the

Committee as desired. Mankind was now often noting these two components as opposing decisions and often discussed by mankind as a decision between heart and mind. The Committee discussed that these two features of mankind (heart and mind) as not meant to be in opposition but that was and is again a free will decision by mankind.

**Recent Attention Attempts:** During the time of the mystery age with a flexible time length the Word had indicated this time period in several direct scriptures. The Committee noted that fixed time in prophesy cannot be changed for prophesy is set. Hence, the Committee noted that the flexible time length could change based on mankind's ignoring of the opportunity available. (This decision of the Committee to shorten time in the seventieth week is indicated in the Word. Likewise, the time for the rapture is considered to be imminent by inspired mankind and by the Committee.)

> Mathew 24:22 kjv 22And except those days should be **shortened**, there should no flesh be saved: but for the elect's sake those days shall be **shortened**.

> Romans 9:28 kjv 28For he will finish the work, and cut it short in righteousness: because a short work will the Lord make upon the earth.

Before discussing the determination of the time of rapture, the Committee decided to rehearse the times that had now passed in setting up the current foundation of their plan from the beginning of the first covenant through prophecy of nations and Jesus and the mystery age beyond prophecy. The following is their historical summary as already revealed in the Word.

The Committee noted that the final decision of destiny was an individual decision based on the free will of each of mankind as it had been for Abraham. True believers in Israel (present, past, and future) would be saved and used in the final days. The previous inspired writers of the Word had been Israelites. Thus, as planned, the Word had been provided by the Israelites through the Word and continued to be so. This had always been the plan (through prophecy and through mystery). **_All the Word had been written by the Israelites, so the Israelites had actually spread the Word as intended . . . and many mankind had thought the Israelites had failed to spread the Word._** Mankind had misinterpreted how the Committee planned for their own free will decisions to be accomplished. Even Israel has not recognized that Israelites had spread the Word as planned . . . The blindness of the Israelites had not interfered with the plan of the Committee to have the Israelites spread the Word.

**_What to Expect in the Future:_** The Committee knew that they had some duties to continue. They discussed prophetic fulfillment of the end time and what mankind should expect. Mankind should expect continued literal fulfillment of the prophecies found in the Word. The fulfillment of previous prophecies had been literal when mankind thought them impossible. The Committee could not help but recall great examples that recently happened. (After all, the Committee could not help but wonder at mankind's failure to follow the Committee's plan as developed and now being removed from out of the shadows to show reality of the truths found in the Word.) Mankind should begin to pay attention. Literal events such as the Israelite nation being reestablished with the Jews returning as prophesied, the beginning establishment of Jerusalem as the capital, the involvement of the United States in development of Israel as a nation under President Truman and later the capital of Jerusalem by President Trump, and current peace agreements in the middle east serve as examples for mankind to ponder. These recent movements that happened through movement of world events was similar to the fulfillment of Micah 5:2 in the Word. In this latter case, Jesus was born in Bethlehem Ephratah as prophesied approximately 700 years before through directions of Augustus Caesar to collect taxes (Luke 2:1-6) prophesy was amazingly fulfilled. The Committee noted the setting of carrying out of literal plans through sequential world movements. They discussed the setup of getting the prophesy of Jesus being born in Bethlehem Ephratah through several hundreds of years and how mankind should piece together the shadows (clues) of the Word to see use of their foreknowledge.

> Isaiah 11:1-4 kjv 1 And there shall come forth a rod out of the **stem of Jesse**, and a **Branch** shall grow out of his roots: 2 And the spirit of the LORD shall rest upon him, the spirit of wisdom and understanding, the spirit of counsel and might, the spirit of knowledge and of the fear of the LORD; 3 And shall make him of quick understanding in the fear of the LORD: and he shall not judge after the sight of his eyes, neither reprove after the hearing of his ears: 4 But

with righteousness shall he judge the poor, and reprove with equity for the meek of the earth: and he shall smite the earth: with the rod of his mouth, and with the breath of his lips shall he slay the wicked.

Micah 5:1 kjv 2 But thou, Bethlehem Ephratah, though thou be little among the thousands of Judah, yet out of thee shall he come forth unto me that is to be ruler in Israel; whose goings forth have been from of old, from everlasting.

I Samuel 17:12 kjv 12 Now **David** *was the son of that Ephrathite of Bethlehem-judah, whose name was* **Jesse;** and he had eight sons: and the man went among men for an old man in the days of Saul.

Luke 2:1-6 kjv 1 And it came to pass in those days, that there went out a *decree from Caesar Augustus that all the world should be taxed.* 2 (And this taxing was first made when Cyrenius was governor of Syria.) 3 And all went to be taxed, every one into his own city. 4 And **Joseph** also went up from Galilee, out of the city of Nazareth, into Judaea, *unto the city of David, which is called Bethlehem;* (because he was of the house and lineage of David:) 5 To be taxed with **Mary** his espoused wife, being great with child. 6 And so it was, that, while they were there, the days were accomplished that she should be delivered.

A similar sequence of world movements including the outcome of a world war is to be found by mankind in support of understanding the setup of the Committee to fulfill the reestablishment of the nation of Israel in prophecy. The literal fulfillment to continue remains intact as time continues. The kingdom of Jacob is to come with Jesus and David in place as predicted.

The Committee noted the telling of special events in the life of Jesus before He was born. The Committee wondered if mankind realized that mankind could not tell ahead of time when, where, and how mankind would be born. Neither could mankind tell when, where, and how mankind would die. (How could the Committee do that about Jesus?) Why a virgin birth? should now be evident to mankind based on the Committee's meeting and revealing some of the hidden meanings intended to be recognized as hidden but being revealed through time.

The Committee adjourned the meeting to observe continued fulfillment as mankind used and abused the understanding for the truth as divided in the Word. The lack of mankind to simply understand the warning that nations that violated the original placement of Israel in prophecy has been and is to be destroyed was hard for the Committee to understand. Proof is presented with the witness of three as needed . . . the Committee itself exists as three.

> Matthew18:16 kjv 16 But if he will not hear thee, then take with thee one or two more, that in the mouth of two or three **witnesses** every word may be established.

> 1 John 5:6-9 kjv 6 This is he that came by water and blood, even Jesus Christ; not by water only, but by water and blood. And it is the Spirit that beareth witness because the Spirit is truth. 7 For <u>there are three that bear record in heaven, the Father, the Word, and</u>

*the Holy Ghost*: and these three are one. ⁸And there are *three that bear witness in earth, the Spirit, and the water, and the blood*: and these three agree in one. ⁹If we receive the witness of men, the witness of God is greater: for this is the witness of God which he hath testified of his Son.

As in the beginning: The Committee planned the created *heavens and the earth* . . . this division is consistent and remains through the end representing the *invisible and the visible*.

**The End of the Review:** The Committee had spent a lot of this meeting in review and discussion as they considered the development of their plan recorded in the Word. They had considered a part of their planned revealed truths for mankind to be able to understand. They knew that all that they had planned and had done for mankind could not be recorded in books. Just what the One in the glorified body had done by Himself could not be recorded in books as indicated in the Word. However, the Word had been reviewed and was noted as complete.

<sub>John 21:25 kjv 25</sub>And there are also many other things which Jesus did, the which, if they should be written every one, I suppose that even the world itself could not contain the books that should be written. Amen.

**Time for a Decision: The Committee knew that the time had come to make a decision that had to be made. They had made a similar decision many times before and had continued to record the** past decisions in the Word and mankind was now approaching a point of no return. The Committee recognized this point and noted the end was near if not already present. The Committee's free will decision to be made was clear as stated in the Word. They had to choose between the longsuffering extension of the flexible time of grace (the mystery time) based on the sign of Jonah or the cutting short of the flexible time of grace (the mystery time) based on the sign of Noah. The decision had been made in the time of Noah and mankind was again approaching the world social environment being as it was in the days of Noah. The time of the final promise of wrath on the earth continued to approach as the birth pains of travail for earth continued to get closer and closer together. The convergence of signs mentioned earlier evidenced the closeness of birth pains for mankind to consider. (These birth pains of Israel coming after the birth of Israel was another mystery shadow of Israel being revealed. Also, noteworthy for mankind is the birth pains of the old earth.)

The Committee finished this meeting with a firm feeling that their plan had been, was, and would continue with the success that had been determined in the beginning. They had seen that mankind had performed as expected. The consequences of performance by mankind had been planned and decisions had been, were being made, and would continue to be made as planned based on foreknowledge of the free will decisions of mankind. The wide road was now almost full, and the narrow road was too. The city cube of Revelations was finished and ready for use and did house the correct number of mansions according to foreknowledge. The pains of birth by the

Earth was observed more and more each day but not recognized as such by most of mankind. A statement by mankind had been made that mother earth was angry when in truth mankind should begin to realize that Father God was the one to fear. The Committee had completed their review for this meeting. The Committee agreed on a decision. One was still seated and made the decision that the others agreed on for now, One had a little work to do, and the third One with the glorified body was no longer sitting by the Father's right side but was now standing . . . but there were a few more books to complete . . . some names were to be added and some to be blotted out . . . as free will decisions by present generations of mankind were still being made , , , <u>but the book containing the Word was complete. Works alone would not save. As with Abraham and ALL, belief in the Committee and established faith was needed to not be dead and to be born again. Longsuffering was temporarily extended. However, the foundation for beginning the end week of Daniel's seventy-week prophesy was considered imminent by the Committee in tune with the ending of the current age of mystery. Works alone was and are considered dead based on substance of things hoped for and evidence of things unseen by shadows seen. The Committee noted that mankind does not want to be judged by works alone as faith goes beyond works.</u>

<sub>Revelation 20:12 kjv</sub> 12And I saw the dead, small and great, stand before God; and the books were opened: and another book was opened, which is the book of life: and the dead were judged out of those things

which were written in the books, according to their works.

The Committee adjourned for now with an intent to meet again as the major decision depended as it had in the destruction of Sodom and Gomorrah. The extension depended on the existence of mankind providing glorification of the Committee with the Committee recognition that the end would come as it had with Sodom and Gomorrah.

<sub>Genesis 18:20-33 kjv</sub> 20 And the LORD said, Because the cry of Sodom and Gomorrah is great, and because their sin is very grievous; 21 I will go down now, and see whether they have done altogether according to the cry of it, which is come unto me; and if not, I will know. 22 And the men turned their faces from thence, and went toward Sodom: but Abraham stood yet before the LORD. 23 And Abraham drew near, and said, *Wilt thou also destroy the righteous with the wicked?* 24 Peradventure there be fifty righteous within the city: wilt thou also destroy and not spare the place for the fifty righteous that are therein? 25 That be far from thee to do after this manner, to slay the righteous with the wicked: and that the righteous should be as the wicked, that be far from thee: *Shall not the Judge of all the earth do right?* 26 And the LORD said, If I find in Sodom fifty righteous within the city, then I will spare all the place for their sakes. 27 And Abraham answered and said, Behold now, I have taken upon me to speak unto the LORD, which am but dust and ashes:

²⁸ Peradventure there shall lack five of the fifty righteous: wilt thou destroy all the city for lack of five? And he said, If I find there forty and five, I will not destroy it. ²⁹ And he spake unto him yet again, and said, peradventure there shall be forty found there. And he said, I will not do it for forty's sake. ³⁰ And he said unto him, Oh let not the LORD be angry, and I will speak: Peradventure there shall thirty be found there. And he said, I will not do it, if I find thirty there. ³¹ And he said, Behold now, I have taken upon me to speak unto the LORD: Peradventure there shall be twenty found there. And he said, I will not destroy it for twenty's sake. ³² And he said, Oh let not the LORD be angry, and I will speak yet but this once: Peradventure ten shall be found there. And he said, I will not destroy it for ten's sake. ³³ And the LORD went his way as soon as he had left communing with Abraham: and Abraham returned unto his place.

The Committee finished with a final truth for the end times as indicated in the Word and recorded in Genesis 18. None of the righteous (Gentile individuals or Israelite individuals) would be left as dead. However, as in the time of Sodom and Gomorrah the rapture and events of the end is determined by the free will of mankind and his glorification of the Committee through belief in the finished work of the Son. Mankind free will decisions will determine the times being as in the times of Noah as they did in the times of Noah. (The Committee again noted that counting the righteous and counting the unrighteous was actually the same counting. To mankind, this was a mystery that revealed a truth.)

All mankind now faced the same opportunity that the Israelites had faced at least twice. Mankind could now acknowledge *the sign of Jonah* and extend the flexible time of the mystery age by appropriate belief in the truth or continue to create the society of mankind reflecting the *sign of Noah* bringing in the fixed time of the seventieth week. The Committee discussed that mankind had a great opportunity to show their compassion as the Committee had in longsuffering in extending the age. Although misunderstood as shown in the Word, an extension of the flexible time would give other mankind more time to understand and accept the true sacrifice through appropriate faith and belief. Extension of the mystery age was the choice that the Committee agreed and stressed as being the way they wanted. However, they knew by their foreknowledge that in the long run a majority of mankind would of their own free will bring in the times as in the day of Noah. The determination to end the transition into the seventieth week and the imminent harvest of believers has always been and is in the mind of the Father. However, the Committee had now discussed the flexible length of time until the seventieth week of Daniel revealing many truths **out of the shadows**.

**A Parting Shadow:** As the Committee parted from the meeting, the Committee noted the time of mystery still contained new and continuing shadows to be revealed. One of extreme meaning was similar to the narrow road and the wide road often mentioned by mankind.

264

*Mystery Shadow of Narrow Road:* In order for a narrow road there must be a comparison. Hence a wider road is to be considered. The Committee noted that in the Word, a narrow road is presented. Of Necessity for comparison there needs to be a wider road. The Word presents the narrow road representing mankind in belief accepting Jesus for the salvation of the Jews for Jews and Gentiles. The wide road represents mankind in unbelief and not accepting Jesus and the salvation plan discussed in the Word. In the present age the Committee discussed a mystery shadow that is now leading into a great delusion as discussed in the Word.

<sub>John 4:22 kjv 22</sub>Ye worship ye know not what: we know what we worship: for salvation is of the Jews.

<sub>Matthew 7:13-14 kjv 13</sub>Enter ye in at the strait gate: for wide is the gate, and broad is the way, that leadeth to destruction, and many there be which go in thereat: Because strait is the gate, and narrow is the way, which leadeth unto life, and few there be that find it.

*A shadow of rejection* of the Committee has been shown in the Word. *This rejection was by Israel* as they were ready to enter the promised land for the first time. The narrow road was represented by two out of a few (twelve) that had faith. These two (Joshua and Caleb) were the only ones of the few (twelve) that got to enter the promised land. The wide road was represented by ten of the few (twelve). These ten did not get to enter the promised land.

<sub>Numbers 14:30 kjv 30</sub>Doubtless ye shall not come into the land, concerning which I sware to make you dwell therein, save Caleb the son of Jephunneh, and Joshua the son of Nun.

*A current mystery shadow of rejection* of the Committee is being shown in the World. *This rejection mystery shadow is being shown in the United States* as all mankind approaches the end time. The narrow road of truth is presented by two of a few. The wide road of destruction is presented by a majority of the few.

**An Important Historical Event:** *The United States as a nation (due to individual free-will voting decisions) will make a major determination for support of the Word in 2020 or perhaps in 2024 or later. The nation will support Israel or will decide to enter a time of the curse announced by the Word in the Abrahamic covenant.*

**A Parting Comment:** *From the Committee: Shadows need light to form. Without light there are no shadows . . . just darkness.*

Current References of Truth

Considered to be among approved truths by the Committee

by the author.

(Always compare with the true standard.)

    1. The King James Version of the Word (the true standard!)

2. Presentations of "End of the Age" by Dr. Irven Baxter as one dedicated to prophecy being fulfilled in the seventieth week.
3. Presentations of "Through the Bible" by Les Feldick, a truth teaching rancher from Oklahoma.
4. Presentations of "Hagee Ministries" by John and Matt Hagee. ministers of the truth from the Word.
5. Presentations of "Turning Point" by Dr. David Jeremiah, preaching the Truth of the Word.
6. Presentations of "Forgotten Truths" by Dr. Richard Jordan, President of Grace School of Bible, currently presenting the right division of truth in the bible.
7. Presentations of "Lamb and Lion Ministries" by Dr. David Reagen, in "Christ in Prophecy" proclaiming the soon return of Jesus.
8. Presentations of "Manna-Fest" with Perry Stone, an informative interpretation of the Word.
9. Presentations of "Sonlight Broadcasting Network" and "Family Worship Center" by Jimmy Swaggert, Donnie Swaggert, and Gabrial Swaggert, dedicated to revealing the true meaning of Sonlight from the perspective of the cross.

Out of the Shadows

www.ingramcontent.com/pod-product-compliance
Lightning Source LLC
Chambersburg PA
CBHW022111040426
42450CB00006B/660